Exxon: The Road Not Taken

By Neela Banerjee

John H. Cushman Jr.

David Hasemyer

and Lisa Song

OTHER TITLES

CONTENTS

INTRODUCTION

Laura Shaw was 12 years old when she won her seventh-grade science fair at the Solomon Schechter Day School in Cranford, N.J. with a project on the greenhouse effect. It was 1981, and no one at her school was even aware of it.

Laura knew about it well because her father was an Exxon scientist, and he had schooled his daughter on the emerging problem that her generation is now inheriting.

The company at that time was at the forefront of climate research, long before the general public knew about climate change.

This surprising detail is one of many that you'll find in the following pages, a compilation of the nine articles in our groundbreaking investigative series called Exxon: The Road Not Taken.

It's a brief history of Exxon's engagement with the science of climate change. The story spans four decades, and is based on interviews with former company employees, internal company files never before seen and other evidence.

It describes how Exxon conducted cutting-edge climate research decades ago and pivoted to the forefront of climate denial, manufacturing doubt about the scientific consensus that its own scientists had confirmed.

It is a timely, important and troubling account that is already changing the global conversation about climate change. It is raising questions about Exxon's moral and legal responsibility for the environmental crisis afflicting the entire planet.

Our reporters are continuing to cover unfolding events, and you can follow their work on InsideClimate News. These pages provide the essential background reading.

David Sassoon, Publisher
InsideClimate News

1. EXXON'S OWN RESEARCH CONFIRMED FOSSIL FUELS' ROLE IN GLOBAL WARMING DECADES AGO

Top executives were warned of possible catastrophe from greenhouse effect, then led efforts to block solutions.

By Neela Banerjee, Lisa Song and David Hasemyer

Sept. 21, 2015

At a meeting in Exxon Corporation's headquarters, a senior company scientist named James F. Black addressed an audience of powerful oilmen. Speaking without a text as he flipped through detailed slides, Black delivered a sobering message: carbon dioxide from the world's use of fossil fuels would warm the planet and could eventually endanger humanity.

"In the first place, there is general scientific agreement that the most likely manner in which mankind is influencing the global climate is through carbon dioxide release from the burning of fossil fuels," Black told Exxon's Management Committee, according to a written version he recorded later.

It was July 1977 when Exxon's leaders received this blunt assessment, well before most of the world had heard of the looming climate crisis.

A year later, Black, a top technical expert in Exxon's Research & Engineering division, took an updated version of his presentation to a broader audience. He warned Exxon scientists and managers that independent researchers estimated a doubling of the carbon dioxide (CO_2) concentration in the atmosphere would increase average global temperatures by 2 to 3 degrees Celsius (4 to 5 degrees Fahrenheit), and as much as 10 degrees Celsius (18 degrees Fahrenheit) at the poles. Rainfall might get heavier in some regions, and other places might turn to desert.

"Some countries would benefit but others would have their agricultural output reduced or destroyed," Black said, in the written summary of his 1978 talk.

His presentations reflected uncertainty running through scientific circles about the details of climate change, such as the role the oceans played in absorbing emissions. Still, Black estimated quick action was needed. "Present thinking," he wrote in the 1978 summary, "holds that man has a time window of five to ten years before the need for hard decisions regarding changes in energy strategies might become critical."

Exxon responded swiftly. Within months the company launched its own extraordinary research into carbon dioxide from fossil fuels and its impact on the earth. Exxon's ambitious program included both empirical CO_2 sampling and rigorous climate modeling. It assembled a brain trust that would spend more than a decade deepening the company's understanding of an environmental problem that posed an existential threat to the oil business.

Then, toward the end of the 1980s, Exxon curtailed its carbon dioxide research. In the decades that followed, Exxon worked instead at the forefront of climate denial. It put its muscle behind efforts to manufacture doubt about the reality of global warming its own scientists had once confirmed. It lobbied to block federal and international action to control greenhouse gas emissions. It helped to erect a vast edifice of misinformation that stands to this day.

This untold chapter in Exxon's history, when one of the world's largest energy companies worked to understand the damage caused by fossil fuels, stems from an eight-month investigation by InsideClimate News. ICN's reporters interviewed former Exxon employees, scientists, and federal officials, and consulted hundreds of pages of internal Exxon documents, many of them written between 1977 and 1986, during the heyday of Exxon's innovative climate research program. ICN combed through thousands of documents from archives including those held at the University of Texas-Austin, the Massachusetts Institute of Technology and the American Association for the Advancement of Science.

The documents record budget requests, research priorities, and debates over findings, and reveal the arc of Exxon's internal attitudes and work on climate and how much attention the results received.

Of particular significance was a project launched in August 1979, when the company outfitted a supertanker with custom-made instruments. The project's mission was to sample carbon dioxide in the air and ocean along a route from the Gulf of Mexico to the Persian Gulf.

In 1980, Exxon assembled a team of climate modelers who investigated fundamental questions about the climate's sensitivity to the buildup of carbon dioxide in the air. Working with university scientists and the U.S. Department of Energy, Exxon strove to be on the cutting edge of inquiry into what was then called the greenhouse effect.

Exxon's early determination to understand rising carbon dioxide levels grew out of a corporate culture of farsightedness, former employees said. They described a company that continuously examined risks to its bottom line, including environmental factors. In the 1970s, Exxon modeled its research division after Bell Labs, staffing it with highly accomplished scientists and engineers.

In written responses to questions about the history of its research, ExxonMobil spokesman Richard D. Keil said that "from the time that climate change first emerged as a topic for scientific study and analysis in the late 1970s, ExxonMobil has committed itself to scientific, fact-based analysis of this important issue."

"At all times," he said, "the opinions and conclusions of our scientists and researchers on this topic have been solidly within the mainstream of the consensus scientific opinion of the day and our work has been guided by an overarching principle to follow where the science leads. The risk of climate change is real and warrants action."

At the outset of its climate investigations almost four decades ago, many Exxon executives, middle managers and scientists armed themselves with a sense of urgency and mission.

One manager at Exxon Research, Harold N. Weinberg, shared his "grandiose thoughts" about Exxon's potential role in climate research in a March 1978 internal company memorandum that read: "This may be the kind of opportunity that we are looking for to have Exxon technology, management and leadership resources put into the context of a project aimed at benefitting mankind."

His sentiment was echoed by Henry Shaw, the scientist leading the company's nascent carbon dioxide research effort.

"Exxon must develop a credible scientific team that can critically evaluate the information generated on the subject and be able to carry bad news, if any, to the corporation," Shaw wrote to his boss Edward E. David, the president of Exxon Research and Engineering in 1978. "This team must be recognized for its excellence in the scientific community, the government, and internally by Exxon management."

IRREVERSIBLE AND CATASTROPHIC

Exxon budgeted more than $1 million over three years for the tanker

3

project to measure how quickly the oceans were taking in CO_2. It was a small fraction of Exxon Research's annual $300 million budget, but the question the scientists tackled was one of the biggest uncertainties in climate science: how quickly could the deep oceans absorb atmospheric CO_2? If Exxon could pinpoint the answer, it would know how long it had before CO_2 accumulation in the atmosphere could force a transition away from fossil fuels.

Exxon also hired scientists and mathematicians to develop better climate models and publish research results in peer-reviewed journals. By 1982, the company's own scientists, collaborating with outside researchers, created rigorous climate models – computer programs that simulate the workings of the climate to assess the impact of emissions on global temperatures. They confirmed an emerging scientific consensus that warming could be even worse than Black had warned five years earlier.

Exxon's research laid the groundwork for a 1982 corporate primer on carbon dioxide and climate change prepared by its environmental affairs office. Marked "not to be distributed externally," it contained information that "has been given wide circulation to Exxon management." In it, the company recognized, despite the many lingering unknowns, that heading off global warming "would require major reductions in fossil fuel combustion."

Unless that happened, "there are some potentially catastrophic events that must be considered," the primer said, citing independent experts. "Once the effects are measurable, they might not be reversible."

THE CERTAINTY OF UNCERTAINTY

Like others in the scientific community, Exxon researchers acknowledged the uncertainties surrounding many aspects of climate science, especially in the area of forecasting models. But they saw those uncertainties as questions they wanted to address, not an excuse to dismiss what was increasingly understood.

"Models are controversial," Roger Cohen, head of theoretical sciences at Exxon Corporate Research Laboratories, and his colleague, Richard Werthamer, senior technology advisor at Exxon Corporation, wrote in a May 1980 status report on Exxon's climate modeling program. "Therefore, there are research opportunities for us."

When Exxon's researchers confirmed information the company might find troubling, they did not sweep it under the rug.

"Over the past several years a clear scientific consensus has emerged," Cohen wrote in September 1982, reporting on Exxon's own analysis of climate models. It was that a doubling of the carbon dioxide blanket in the atmosphere would produce average global warming of 3 degrees Celsius, plus or minus 1.5 degrees C (equal to 5 degrees Fahrenheit plus or minus 1.7 degrees F).

"There is unanimous agreement in the scientific community that a temperature increase of this magnitude would bring about significant changes in the earth's climate," he wrote, "including rainfall distribution and alterations in the biosphere."

He warned that publication of the company's conclusions might attract media attention because of the "connection between Exxon's major business and the role of fossil fuel combustion in contributing to the increase of atmospheric CO_2."

Nevertheless, he recommended publication.

Our "ethical responsibility is to permit the publication of our research in the scientific literature," Cohen wrote. "Indeed, to do otherwise would be a breach of Exxon's public position and ethical credo on honesty and integrity."

Exxon followed his advice. Between 1983 and 1984, its researchers published their results in at least three peer-reviewed papers in *Journal of the Atmospheric Sciences* and an American Geophysical Union monograph.

David, the head of Exxon Research, told a global warming conference financed by Exxon in October 1982 that "few people doubt that the world has entered an energy transition away from dependence upon fossil fuels and toward some mix of renewable resources that will not pose problems of CO_2 accumulation." The only question, he said, was how fast this would happen.

But the challenge did not daunt him. "I'm generally upbeat about the chances of coming through this most adventurous of all human experiments with the ecosystem," David said.

Exxon considered itself unique among corporations for its carbon dioxide and climate research. The company boasted in a January 1981 report, "Scoping Study on CO_2," that no other company appeared to be conducting similar in-house research into carbon dioxide, and it swiftly gained a reputation among outsiders for genuine expertise.

"We are very pleased with Exxon's research intentions related to the CO_2 question. This represents very responsible action, which we hope will serve as a model for research contributions from the corporate sector," said David Slade, manager of the federal government's carbon dioxide research program at the Energy Department, in a May 1979 letter to Shaw. "This is truly a national and international service.".

BUSINESS IMPERATIVES

In the early 1980s Exxon researchers often repeated that unbiased science would give it legitimacy in helping shape climate-related laws that would affect its profitability.

Still, corporate executives remained cautious about what they told Exxon's shareholders about global warming and the role petroleum played in causing it, a review of federal filings shows. The company did not elaborate on the carbon problem in annual reports filed with securities regulators during the height of its CO_2 research.

Nor did it mention in those filings that concern over CO_2 was beginning to influence business decisions it was facing.

Throughout the 1980s, the company was worried about developing an enormous gas field off the coast of Indonesia because of the vast amount of CO_2 the unusual reservoir would release.

Exxon was also concerned about reports that synthetic oil made from coal, tar sands and oil shales could significantly boost CO_2 emissions. The company was banking on synfuels to meet growing demand for energy in the future, in a world it believed was running out of conventional oil.

In the mid-1980s, after an unexpected oil glut caused prices to collapse, Exxon cut its staff deeply to save money, including many working on climate. But the climate change problem remained, and it was becoming a more prominent part of the political landscape.

"Global Warming Has Begun, Expert Tells Senate," declared the headline of a June 1988 New York Times article describing the Congressional testimony of NASA's James Hansen, a leading climate expert. Hansen's statements compelled Sen. Tim Wirth (D-Colo.) to declare during the hearing that "Congress must begin to consider how we are going to slow or halt that warming trend."

With alarm bells suddenly ringing, Exxon started financing efforts to amplify doubt about the state of climate science.

Exxon helped to found and lead the Global Climate Coalition, an alliance of some of the world's largest companies seeking to halt government efforts to curb fossil fuel emissions. Exxon used the American Petroleum Institute, right-wing think tanks, campaign contributions and its own lobbying to push a narrative that climate science was too uncertain to necessitate cuts in fossil fuel emissions.

As the international community moved in 1997 to take a first step in curbing emissions with the Kyoto Protocol, Exxon's chairman and CEO Lee Raymond argued to stop it.

"Let's agree there's a lot we really don't know about how climate will change in the 21st century and beyond," Raymond said in his speech before

6

the World Petroleum Congress in Beijing in October 1997.

"We need to understand the issue better, and fortunately, we have time," he said. "It is highly unlikely that the temperature in the middle of the next century will be significantly affected whether policies are enacted now or 20 years from now."

Over the years, several Exxon scientists who had confirmed the climate consensus during its early research, including Cohen and David, took Raymond's side, publishing views that ran contrary to the scientific mainstream.

PAYING THE PRICE

Exxon's about-face on climate change earned the scorn of the scientific establishment it had once courted.

In 2006, the Royal Society, the United Kingdom's science academy, sent a harsh letter to Exxon accusing it of being "inaccurate and misleading" on the question of climate uncertainty. Bob Ward, the Academy's senior manager for policy communication, demanded that Exxon stop giving money to dozens of organizations he said were actively distorting the science.

In 2008, under mounting pressure from activist shareholders, the company announced it would end support for some prominent groups such as those Ward had identified.

Still, the millions of dollars Exxon had spent since the 1990s on climate change deniers had long surpassed what it had once invested in its path-breaking climate science aboard the *Esso Atlantic*.

"They spent so much money and they were the only company that did this kind of research as far as I know," Edward Garvey, who was a key researcher on Exxon's oil tanker project, said in a recent interview with InsideClimate News and Frontline. "That was an opportunity not just to get a place at the table, but to lead, in many respects, some of the discussion. And the fact that they chose not to do that into the future is a sad point."

Michael Mann, director of the Earth System Science Center at Pennsylvania State University, who has been a frequent target of climate deniers, said that inaction, just like actions, have consequences. When he recently spoke to InsideClimate News, he was unaware of this chapter in Exxon's history.

"All it would've taken is for one prominent fossil fuel CEO to know this was about more than just shareholder profits, and a question about our legacy," he said. "But now because of the cost of inaction—what I call the 'procrastination penalty'—we face a far more uphill battle."

7

ICN staff members Zahra Hirji, Paul Horn, Naveena Sadasivam, Sabrina Shankman and Alexander Wood also contributed to this report.

"In the first place, there is general scientific agreement that the most likely manner in which mankind is influencing the global climate is through carbon dioxide release from the burning of fossil fuels."

James F. Black
Exxon Senior Scientist
1978

"Currently, the scientific evidence is inconclusive as to whether human activities are having a significant effect on the global climate."

Lee Raymond
Exxon Chairman and CEO
1997

2. EXXON BELIEVED DEEP DIVE INTO CLIMATE RESEARCH WOULD PROTECT ITS BUSINESS

Outfitting its biggest supertanker to measure the ocean's absorption of carbon dioxide was a crown jewel in Exxon's research program.

By Neela Banerjee, Lisa Song and David Hasemyer

Sept. 21, 2015

In 1981, 12-year-old Laura Shaw won her seventh-grade science fair at the Solomon Schechter Day School in Cranford, N.J. with a project on the greenhouse effect.

For her experiment, Laura used two souvenir miniatures of the Washington Monument, each with a thermometer attached to one side. She placed them in glass bowls and covered one with plastic wrap – her model of how a blanket of carbon dioxide traps the reflected heat of the sun and warms the Earth. When she turned a lamp on them, the thermometer in the plastic-covered bowl showed a higher temperature than the one in the uncovered bowl.

If Laura and her two younger siblings were unusually well-versed in the emerging science of the greenhouse effect, as global warming was known, it was because their father, Henry Shaw, had been busily tracking it for Exxon Corporation.

"I knew what the greenhouse effect was before I knew what an actual greenhouse was," David Shaw, Henry's son, said in a recent interview.

Henry Shaw, who died in 2003, was one of the Exxon scientists engaged in an ambitious quest to comprehend the potentially devastating effects that carbon dioxide emissions could have on the climate. From the late 1970s to the mid-80s, Exxon scientists worked at the cutting edge of climate change research, documents examined by InsideClimate News show. This history of that research emerged from an eight-month investigation by InsideClimate News.

Exxon documents show that top corporate managers were aware of their scientists' early conclusions about carbon dioxide's impact on the climate. They reveal that scientists warned management that policy changes to address climate change might affect profitability. After a decade of frank internal discussions on global warming and conducting unbiased studies on it, Exxon changed direction in 1989 and spent more than 20 years discrediting the research its own scientists had once confirmed.

After reading the first chapter of InsideClimate News' series on Exxon's carbon dioxide research, the company declined to answer specific questions. In an email, Exxon spokesman Richard D. Keil said he would no longer respond to inquiries from InsideClimate News, and added, "ExxonMobil scientists have been involved in climate research and related policy analysis for more than 30 years, yielding more than 50 papers in peer-reviewed publications."

BUILDING THE TEAM

Henry Shaw was part of an accomplished group at Exxon tasked with studying the greenhouse effect. In the mid-70s, documents show that Shaw was responsible for seeking out new projects that were "of national significance," and that could win federal funding. Others included Edward E. David, Jr., a former science advisor to President Richard Nixon, and James F. Black, who worked on hydrogen bomb research at Oak Ridge National Laboratory in the 1950s.

Black, who died in 1988, was among the first Exxon scientists to become acquainted with the greenhouse effect. Esso, as Exxon was known when he started, allowed him to pursue personal scientific interests. Black was fascinated by the idea of intentionally modifying weather to improve agriculture in arid countries, said his daughter, Claudia Black-Kalinsky.

"He believed that big science could save the world," she said. In the early 1960s, Black helped draft a National Academy of Sciences report on weather and climate modification. Published in 1966, it said the buildup of carbon dioxide in the atmosphere "agrees quite well with the rate of its production by man's consumption of fossil fuels."

In the same period, a report for President Lyndon Johnson from the

President's Science Advisory Council in 1965 said the burning of fossil fuels "may be sufficient to produce measurable and perhaps marked changes in climate" by the year 2000.

By 1977, Black had become a top technical expert at Exxon Research & Engineering, a research hub based in Linden, N.J., and a science advisor to Exxon's top management. That year he made a presentation to the company's leading executives warning that carbon dioxide accumulating in the upper atmosphere would warm the planet and if the CO_2 concentration continued to rise, it could harm the environment and humankind.

"The management committee consisted of the top level senior managers at Exxon. The chairman, the president, the senior vice presidents, corporate wide," N. Richard Werthamer, who worked at Exxon Research, said in a recent interview with InsideClimate News. "The management committee only has a limited amount of time and they're only going to deal with issues that are of relevance to the corporation as a whole. They're not interested in science per se, they are interested in the implications, so it was very significant."

In those years, the evidence of global warming justified neither panic nor complacency. "A lively sense of urgency," is what the National Academy of Sciences (NAS) called for in a 1977 report that contained a comprehensive survey of what was understood about global warming at that time.

The NAS report said that it would be understandable if the uncertainties of climate science elicited a cautious response from researchers and policymakers. But "if the decision is postponed until the impact of man-made climate changes has been felt, then, for all practical purposes, the die will already have been cast," it concluded.

Shaw heard these conclusions in October 1977 at a meeting in Atlanta organized by scientists and officials from the Carter administration who had formed a "study group on global environmental effects of carbon dioxide," he told Exxon colleagues in a memo two weeks later.

The NAS report had concluded that the climatic effects of rising carbon dioxide "may be the primary limiting factor on energy production from fossil fuels over the next few centuries," Shaw wrote, quoting the report's central conclusion almost verbatim.

Along with an awareness of the science, Shaw gained a sense of opportunity, Exxon documents show. The U.S. Energy Department, which had only been created in 1977 in response to a global oil shortage, was launching a research program into carbon dioxide's effects and planned to disburse about $9 million to research laboratories, Shaw learned.

At the time, two major uncertainties plagued climate science: how much of the CO_2 in the air came from fossil fuels as opposed to deforestation? And how quickly could the oceans absorb atmospheric CO_2? The scientists at the Atlanta meeting considered it crucial to investigate those questions immediately, Shaw wrote.

Both issues were vital to the oil industry's future. If deforestation played as great a role as fossil fuels in CO_2 accumulation, then responsibility for reducing carbon dioxide emissions would not fall entirely on the energy industry. If the oceans could slow the greenhouse effect by absorbing more CO_2, there would be time before the fossil fuel industry had to adjust.

In a memo to a colleague in March 1978, one of Shaw's bosses, Harold N. Weinberg, wrote: "I propose that Exxon be the initiator of a worldwide 'CO_2 in the Atmosphere' R&D program…What would be more appropriate than for the world's leading energy company and leading oil company [to] take the lead in trying to define whether a long-term CO_2 problem really exists, and if so, what counter measures would be appropriate."

But Weinberg's vision proved too ambitious for Exxon.

Exxon Research "considered an independent research program but concluded that the amount of effort required and the scope of disciplines involved made it impractical for a single institution to attack this problem alone," Walter R. Eckelmann, an executive at the Science & Technology Department at Exxon headquarters in New York wrote to a senior vice president.

Eckelmann's letter was one of many instances when Exxon's CO_2 research would reach beyond Exxon Research & Engineering in New Jersey and to executives at the company's New York headquarters, documents show.

Exxon's extensive research was driven by the threat accumulating CO_2 posed to the company's core business, according to participants and documents.

"My guess is they were looking for what might happen if we keep burning fossil fuels; what that would mean to them," said Taro Takahashi, an adjunct professor at Columbia University's Lamont-Doherty Earth Observatory. Takahashi, who spent his career studying climate change, collaborated on a research project with Exxon in the late 1970s to early 80s and used data from the research in several studies he later published in peer-reviewed journals.

The project he worked on—outfitting an ocean tanker to measure the ocean's absorption of carbon dioxide—was a crown jewel in Exxon's research program.

GROUNDBREAKING EXPERIMENTS

Bold research projects were not uncommon at Exxon, which in the

1970s considered gradually shifting from oil to become a diversified energy company. Through its research units, Exxon explored ways to encourage more efficient consumption of petroleum and a wide range of alternative fuels. After company scientist Elliot Berman found a way to slash the cost of making photovoltaic solar cells by 80 percent, Exxon's chairman Clifton Garvin publicized how he heated his family swimming pool with solar power to show support for energy diversification.

To nudge greater innovation, Garvin hired Edward E. David, Jr. in 1977 to run Exxon Research. David had spent two decades at Bell Labs, a leader in the blue-sky research that led to big leaps in technology, and eventually became its director of research. While serving as Nixon's science advisor from 1970-'73, White House staff taught him about climate science as part of a report on energy and electricity issues, one former staff member recalled.

At Exxon, David opened the door wide to studying carbon dioxide.

In a letter to David and 14 other Exxon Research executives in December 1978, Shaw spelled out why Exxon should take on carbon dioxide research—specifically, with the ambitious ocean-sampling initiative.

"The rationale for Exxon's involvement and commitment of funds and personnel is based on our need to assess the possible impact of the greenhouse effect on Exxon business," Shaw wrote. "Exxon must develop a credible scientific team that can critically evaluate the information generated on the subject and be able to carry bad news, if any, to the corporation.

"We see no better method to acquire the necessary reputation than by attacking one of the major uncertainties in the global CO_2 balance, i.e., the flux to the oceans and providing the necessary data."

Scientists knew the oceans had some ability to absorb CO_2 and potentially neutralize climate change. Any CO_2 that made its way from the atmosphere into the deep oceans—more than 50 to 100 feet below the surface—would be sequestered away for hundreds of years. But they also knew the rate of absorption was limited, and determining the exact rate was crucial for understanding the oceans' ability to delay the greenhouse effect.

EXXON'S FLOATING LAB

Exxon delved into the oceans' role by installing a state-of-the-art lab aboard the *Esso Atlantic,* one of the biggest supertankers of the time.

Exxon planned to gather atmospheric and oceanic CO_2 samples along the *Esso Atlantic's* route from the Gulf of Mexico to the Persian Gulf. If the sensors revealed a deep enough oceanic sink, or absorption, the fossil fuel industry might have more time before it had to make tough decisions about its role in warming the planet.

"We couldn't account for everything because the exchanges between the atmosphere and the oceans weren't fully understood," Edward Garvey, Shaw's main researcher on the tanker project, said in an interview. "Our goal was to complete the carbon cycle to understand where global carbon production would end up and then make forecasts of how the system would react in the future."

The experiment began on August 8, 1979, when Garvey oversaw the equipping of the *Esso Atlantic,* which was docked by the Lago Refinery in Aruba, an island in Dutch West Indies.

Werthamer, Shaw's boss in 1980-81, said the project wouldn't have happened without Shaw's initiative.

"Henry Shaw was a very forceful guy, quiet, he didn't hit you over the head, but he presented his case in ways that made it hard to not agree with it," Werthamer said in a recent interview. "He had the political savvy to put it over and the technical savvy to make it happen."

While the company had the wherewithal to carry out the study on the oceans, it lacked the expertise. So Exxon recruited two experts, Wallace Broecker and Takahashi, his colleague at Columbia University's Lamont-Doherty Geological Observatory.

Takahashi said he made it clear that he and Broecker would not compromise their scientific integrity. "The one condition that was not negotiable was we shall publish our results to the open public no matter the results," he said in an interview.

Exxon scientists and managers involved with the project agreed.

"The tanker project was intended to provide valid, legitimate, scientific data, unassailable hopefully, on key questions in atmospheric chemistry [of] CO_2 emissions," Werthamer said. "Henry's additional goal was to make Exxon a credible participant in that research and in the dialogue that would inevitably follow...He wanted Exxon to be respected as a valid player and have Exxon's opinions solicited, and participate in discussions on policy, rather than have the issue suddenly dumped with Exxon's back turned."

Responding to ICN's questions about the tanker research last week, Exxon spokesman Richard Keil said it "was actually aimed at increasing understanding of the marine carbon cycle – it had nothing to do with CO_2 emissions."

But from the beginning of the research, documents show, its participants described it differently.

In a memo to Harold Weinberg on July 3, 1979, Shaw described in detail the tanker's route and its instruments, explaining that "this will provide information on the possible growth of CO_2 in the atmosphere."

In a November 1979 memo to Weinberg, he wrote, "It behooves us to start a very aggressive defensive program in the indicated areas of atmospheric science and climate because there is a good probability that legislation affecting our business will be passed."

Depending on its findings, the research might provide an escape valve from the carbon problem, or point to some new direction in energy.

The research "could well influence Exxon's view about the long-term attractiveness of coal and synthetics relative to nuclear and solar energy" David wrote in a November 1979 letter to senior vice president George T. Piercy.

Exxon's enthusiasm for the project flagged in the early '80s when federal funds fell through. Exxon Research cancelled the tanker project in 1982, but not before Garvey, Shaw and other company engineers published an initial paper in a highly specialized journal on the project's methodology.

"We were anxious to get the word out that we were doing this study," Garvey said of the paper, which did not reach sweeping conclusions. "The paper was the first of what we hoped to be many papers from the work," he said in a recent email. But the other publications never materialized.

Takahashi later co-authored a study in 1990 partially based on the tanker data that said land-based ecosystems—boreal forests, for example—absorbed more atmospheric CO_2 than the oceans. He used Exxon's tanker records again in 2009, in an updated study that compiled 30 years of oceanic CO_2 data from dozens of reports. This time, his team concluded the oceans absorb only about 20 percent of the CO_2 emitted annually from fossil fuels and other human activities. The paper earned Takahashi a "Champions of the Earth" prize from the United Nations.

Other research ideas that bubbled up in those days were even more imaginative.

Shaw and Garvey sketched out a second project to determine how much carbon dioxide in the atmosphere was attributable to fossil fuels as compared to deforestation. Shaw's team proposed measuring the carbon isotopes—a chemical fingerprint—in 100 bottles of vintage French wine over time. To ensure data quality, they would only sample wine from long-established vineyards that kept careful records of temperatures and growing conditions. In the same file was a New York Times review by wine critic Frank Prial of classic Bordeaux vintages, including a $300 Lafite-Rothschild bottle from 1945.

"The C-isotope studies of biological material also appear useful and novel," David Slade, the head of the Energy Department's carbon dioxide research, wrote to Shaw in a May 1979 letter. "We congratulate (with some envy) Exxon's resourcefulness in selecting aged wines as the biological material."

IMPLICATIONS BECOME CLEARER

As Exxon worked to reduce the uncertainties of climate science, its employees developed a sophisticated understanding of the potential effects of rising CO_2 concentrations, documents show. They understood that the Earth's poles would warm more quickly than the rest of the planet, and how a reduction in ice and snow cover would change the planet's ability to reflect sunlight.

They also discussed among themselves and with corporate executives other potential effects of climate change, including an increase in weeds, pests, and human migration, the documents show.

Some of the company's highest-ranking executives were told of the studies and of estimates about when the impact of global warming might be felt. On November 9, 1979, Edward David wrote a three-page letter to senior vice president Piercy explaining the importance of the ocean investigations.

In January 1980, Science & Technology's Eckelmann wrote to senior vice president M.E.J. "Morey" O'Loughlin that his unit "feels that the build-up of carbon dioxide in the atmosphere is a potentially serious problem requiring the results of a huge worldwide research effort before quantitative predictions can be reached on the probabilities and timing of world climate changes."

Piercy and O'Loughlin seemed particularly interested in following the emerging climate science, internal documents indicate. In a memo to Werthamer and Shaw in June 1980, Weinberg wrote that Piercy "questioned him closely" at an Exxon meeting about the movement of carbon dioxide between the atmosphere and the oceans.

OUTSIDE EXPERTS TAKE NOTICE

During this time, Exxon was building a reputation for expertise on carbon dioxide, prompting government and industry to seek its input on the issue. As early as 1979, the American Petroleum Institute formed a CO_2 and Climate Task Force, and Exxon sent Shaw to the group's meetings as its representative, according to documents. The other industry members were Sohio, Texaco, and Shell. They often met in a conference room at LaGuardia Airport.

Shaw was a regular on advisory committees and government task forces, rubbing shoulders with many leading climate scientists, including NASA's James Hansen and Columbia's Stephen Schneider, whom Exxon even considered as a possible recruit, according to one document.

U.S. government officials expressed their appreciation to Exxon for the company's contributions, calling it a valued partner.

In a letter to Shaw in May 1979, David Slade, the head of the Energy Department's Carbon Dioxide and Climate Research program, wrote: "This represents very responsible action, which we hope will serve as a model for research contributions from the corporate sector."

Two years later, Slade's successor in President Ronald Reagan's administration, Frederick A. Koomanoff, wrote: "We feel that Exxon should be commended for their initiatives to investigate the carbon dioxide issue."

ICN staff members Zahra Hirji, Paul Horn, Naveena Sadasivam, Sabrina Shankman and Alexander Wood also contributed to this report.

"Present thinking holds that man has a time window of five to ten years before the need for hard decisions regarding changes in energy strategies might become critical."

James F. Black
Exxon Senior Scientist
1978

"It is highly unlikely that the temperature in the middle of the next century will be significantly affected whether the policies are enacted now or 20 years from now."

Lee Raymond
Exxon Chairman and CEO
1997

3. EXXON CONFIRMED GLOBAL WARMING CONSENSUS IN 1982 WITH IN-HOUSE CLIMATE MODELS

The company chairman would later mock climate models as unreliable while he campaigned to stop global action to reduce fossil fuel emissions.

By Lisa Song, Neela Banerjee and David Hasemyer

Sept. 22, 2015

Steve Knisely was an intern at Exxon Research and Engineering in the summer of 1979 when a vice president asked him to analyze how global warming might affect fuel use.

"I think this guy was looking for validation that the greenhouse effect should spur some investment in alternative energy that's not bad for the environment," Knisely, now 58 and a partner in a management consulting company, recalled in a recent interview.

Knisely projected that unless fossil fuel use was constrained, there would be "noticeable temperature changes" and 400 parts per million of carbon dioxide (CO_2) in the air by 2010, up from about 280 ppm before the Industrial Revolution. The summer intern's predictions turned out to be very close to the mark.

Knisely even concluded that the fossil fuel industry might need to leave 80 percent of its recoverable reserves in the ground to avoid doubling CO_2 concentrations, a notion now known as the carbon budget. In 2013, the United Nations' Intergovernmental Panel on Climate Change formally endorsed the idea.

"The potential problem is great and urgent," Knisely wrote. "Too little is known at this time to recommend a major U.S. or worldwide change in energy type usage but it is very clear that immediate research is necessary."

The report, which circulated within the company through the early 1980s, reflected Exxon's growing need to understand when the climate implications of increased CO_2 emissions would begin to spur policy changes.

So Exxon (now ExxonMobil) shelved an ambitious but costly program that sampled carbon dioxide in the oceans—the centerpiece of its climate research in the 1970s—as it created its own computerized climate models. The models aimed to simulate how the planet's climate system would react to rising CO_2 levels, relying on a combination of mathematics, physics, and atmospheric science.

Through much of the 1980s, Exxon researchers worked alongside university and government scientists to generate objective climate models that yielded papers published in peer-reviewed journals. Their work confirmed the emerging scientific consensus on global warming's risks.

Yet starting in 1989, Exxon leaders went down a different road. They repeatedly argued that the uncertainty inherent in computer models makes them useless for important policy decisions. Even as the models grew more powerful and reliable, Exxon publicly derided the type of work its own scientists had done. The company continued its involvement with climate research, but its reputation for objectivity began to erode as it campaigned internationally to cast doubt on the science.

This eight-month InsideClimate News investigation details Exxon's early research into global warming, based on hundreds of pages of internal documents and interviews with former employees and scientists. The company declined to provide comment or answer questions for this article.

One scientist who crossed over from academia to Exxon Research was Brian Flannery, an associate professor of astronomy from Harvard and an expert in mathematical modeling. Flannery joined the company in 1980. At about the same time, Exxon hired Andrew Callegari, a mathematics professor at New York University. When the company shifted its focus to modeling in 1981, Callegari became head of the company's CO_2 research, replacing Henry Shaw, who had steered the ocean sampling project.

Callegari approached Martin Hoffert, an old colleague at NYU, to work with the Exxon team as a consultant on modeling. Hoffert jumped at the chance. He was already deeply concerned about the consequences of atmospheric carbon and saw the opportunity as an "all hands on deck" approach to heading off an environmental disaster.

"We were all interested as geek scientists at the time," Hoffert, who is now retired, recalled in a recent interview. "There were no divisions, no agendas."

Flannery and Callegari were "very legitimate research guys," Hoffert said. "We talked about the politics of this stuff a lot, but we always separated the politics from the science."

CLIMATE 'CATASTROPHE' FORESEEN

By 1981, Exxon scientists were no longer questioning whether the buildup of CO_2 would cause the world to heat up. Through their own studies and their participation in government-sponsored conferences, company researchers had concluded that rising CO_2 levels could create catastrophic impacts within the first half of the 21st century if the burning of oil, gas and coal wasn't contained.

"When I arrived there, I was quite surprised to discover that people in the research lab were very aware of the increase in the growth rate of carbon dioxide measurements in Hawaii [at the Mauna Loa observatory]," Morrel H. Cohen, a senior scientist at Exxon Research from 1981 to 1996, said in a recent interview. "They were very aware of the greenhouse effect."

As the researchers alerted Exxon's upper management about the CO_2 problem, the scientists worked to provide better estimates of when the warming trend would create noticeable damage, and how large the impacts might be.

One scientist, Werner Glass, wrote an analysis in 1981 for a senior vice president that said the rise in global temperatures would begin to be noticed in a few decades. But Glass hedged his bet, saying the magnitude of the change would be "well short of catastrophic" in the early years.

Exxon manager Roger Cohen saw things differently.

"I think that this statement may be too reassuring," Cohen, director of the Theoretical and Mathematical Sciences Laboratory at Exxon Research, wrote in an August 18, 1981 memo to Glass.

He called it "distinctly possible" that the projected warming trend after 2030 "will indeed be catastrophic (at least for a substantial fraction of the earth's population)."

Cohen continued: "This is because the global ecosystem in 2030 might still be in a transient, headed for much significant effects after time lags perhaps of the order of decades."

Cohen demonstrated a sophisticated understanding of the climate system. He recognized that even if the impacts were modest in 2030, the world would have locked in enough CO_2 emissions to ensure more severe consequences in subsequent decades. By 2030, he warned, the damage could be irreversible.

UNANIMOUS AGREEMENT

"Over the past several years a clear scientific consensus has emerged regarding the expected climatic effects of increased atmospheric CO_2," Cohen wrote to A.M. Natkin of Exxon Corporation's Science and Technology Office in 1982. "The consensus is that a doubling of atmospheric CO_2 from its pre-industrial revolution value would result in an average global temperature rise of $(3.0 \pm 1.5)°C$." (Equal to $5.4 \pm 2.7°F$).

"There is unanimous agreement in the scientific community that a temperature increase of this magnitude would bring about significant changes in the earth's climate, including rainfall distribution and alterations in the biosphere."

Exxon's own modeling research confirmed this and the company's results were later published in at least three peer-reviewed science articles. Two of them were co-authored by Hoffert, and a third was written entirely by Flannery.

Exxon's modeling experts also explained away the less-dire predictions of a 1979 study led by Reginald Newell, a prominent atmospheric scientist at the Massachusetts Institute of Technology. Newell's model projected that the effects of climate change would not be as severe as most scientists were predicting.

Specifically, Newell and a co-author from the Air Force named Thomas Dopplick challenged the prevailing view that a doubling of the earth's CO_2 blanket would raise temperatures about $3°C$ $(5°F)$– a measure known as climate sensitivity. Instead, they said the earth's true climate sensitivity was roughly less than $1°C$ $(2°F)$.

They based their results on a mechanism called "evaporative buffering," in which excess warming at the equator causes increased evaporation, cooling the planet in the same way that perspiration cools a marathon runner.

Exxon's research team disagreed. Even if the mechanism cooled the equator, the worldwide warming would still be higher, they found, according to the researchers' peer-reviewed studies.

"In summary, the results of our research are in accord with the scientific consensus on the effect of increased atmospheric CO_2 on climate," Cohen wrote in the 1982 letter he sent to Natkin.

Exxon's science turned out to be spot on, and the company's early modeling projections still hold up more than 30 years later, Hoffert said in an email to InsideClimate News. The Arctic's rapid warming and the extreme vulnerability of Antarctica's ice sheets are "consistent with the results of our theory which predicted them before they happened," Hoffert wrote.

Exxon "should be taking credit for their role in developing useful model predictions of the pattern of global warming by their research guys, as opposed to their denialist lobbyists saying global warming from fossil fuel burning doesn't exist or is at best 'unproven,'" he wrote.

SPREADING THE WORD, INTERNALLY

The conclusions of Exxon's climate modeling were being circulated broadly within the company in the 1980s.

Marvin B. Glaser, an Environmental Affairs Manager at Exxon, distributed a 43-page primer on climate change on Nov. 12, 1982.

In a cover letter to 15 Exxon executives and managers, Glaser said the document provided guidance "on the CO_2 'Greenhouse' Effect which is receiving increased attention in both the scientific and popular press as an emerging environmental issue." He continued: "The material has been given wide circulation to Exxon management and is intended to familiarize Exxon personnel with the subject."

"However, it should be restricted to Exxon personnel and not distributed externally," he wrote.

Glaser's primer drew from the best research of the time, including Exxon's, to explain how global temperatures would rise considerably by the end of the 21st century. Because of the warming, "there are some potentially catastrophic events that must be considered," including sea level rise from melting polar ice sheets, according to the document. It noted that some scientific groups were concerned "that once the effects are measurable, they might not be reversible."

Reining in "the greenhouse effect," the primer said, "would require major reductions in fossil fuel combustion."

Yet the report also argued against a rapid shift to non-fossil fuel energy sources, noting that "making significant changes in energy consumption…amid all the scientific uncertainties would be premature in view of the severe impact such moves could have on the world's economies and societies."

Exxon's reputation for conducting serious carbon dioxide research was growing outside the company. Its scientists were frequent participants on industry and government panels.

Flannery, for example, contributed to a multi-volume series of Energy Department reports published in 1985 on the state of climate change science. It concluded that atmospheric carbon dioxide concentrations had already increased by about 25 percent in the past century, and continued use of fossil fuels would lead to substantial temperature increases in the future.

Flannery was the only industry representative among 15 scientists who wrote the volume titled "Projecting the Climatic Effects of Increasing Carbon Dioxide."

Hoffert and Flannery co-authored a chapter that concluded that since the Industrial Revolution the Earth would warm 1°C (or 2°F) by 2000 and rise another 2 to 5°C (4 to 9°F) over the next hundred years.

As it turned out, the world's temperature has risen about 0.8°C (1.4°F) and mainstream scientists continue to predict, with increasing urgency, that if emissions are not curtailed, carbon pollution would lock in warming of as much as 3 to 6°C (or 5 to 11°F) over the next several decades.

QUANTIFYING THE UNCERTAINTY

Throughout its climate modeling phase, Exxon researchers, like outside scientists, grappled with the uncertainties inherent in climate model projections.

"Models are being used to explore physical effects (scenarios) and as a predictive tool," Andrew Callegari said in a Feb. 2, 1984 presentation for colleagues. The "validity of models [are] not established," Callegari wrote. "Complexity of carbon cycle and climate system require many approximations."

Scientists, regulators and Exxon all had to ask themselves: what should be done, given that uncertainty? Should governments and corporations wait for the ambiguities to be resolved before acting to cut fossil fuel emissions? Or should the researchers recommend immediate action because of a preponderance of evidence?

Since then, modeling has become an increasingly useful and reliable tool. The IPCC, the United Nations institution that compiles the scientific consensus on global warming, has issued a series of reports since 1990 based on those models. Each report has grown more certain. By the fifth report in 2013, the IPCC said it was *"extremely likely* that human influence has been the dominant cause of the observed warming since the mid-20th century."

As the consensus grew within the scientific world, Exxon doubled down on the uncertainty. Its campaign to muddy research results placed the company outside the scientific mainstream. Some of the researchers who once led the company's modeling became vocal climate contrarians, among them Brian Flannery and Roger Cohen.

Flannery survived the lay-offs of the mid-1980s that decimated the

Exxon Research staff and rose in the corporate ranks to become the company's chief scientist. He attended IPCC meetings from the outset and by the early 1990s, he emerged as a prominent skeptic of the science he had once conducted.

For example, in a 1999 paper based on a speech to Exxon's European affiliates, Flannery derided the second IPCC assessment that concluded in 1995 that the scientific evidence suggested "a discernible human influence on climate."

"You'll note that this is a very carefully worded statement, recognizing that the jury is still out, especially on any quantifiable connection to human actions," Flannery wrote. "The conclusion does not refer to global warming from increases in greenhouse gases. Indeed, many scientists say that a great deal of uncertainty still needs to be resolved."

The change in Cohen's thinking was also stark, as he acknowledged in 2008. While still at Exxon he was "well convinced, as were most technically trained people, that the IPCC's case for Anthropogenic Global Warming (AGW) is very tight." But he wrote in a 2008 essay for the Science and Public Policy Institute, a climate denial website, that upon closer inspection of the research he found it to be "flimsy."

In 2007, the American Physical Society, the country's largest organization of physicists, adopted a strong statement on climate change that said "The evidence is incontrovertible: Global warming is occurring."

Cohen, an APS fellow, helped lead a campaign to weaken the APS's official position and earlier this year succeeded in stripping out the word 'incontrovertible' from a draft text. APS members will vote on the final language in November.

Flannery and Cohen declined to comment, despite multiple requests.

Exxon's former chairman and CEO, Lee Raymond, took an even tougher line against climate science. Speaking before the World Petroleum Congress in Beijing in 1997, Raymond mocked climate models in an effort to stop the imminent adoption of the Kyoto Protocol, an international accord to reduce emissions.

"They are notoriously inaccurate," Raymond said. "1990's models were predicting temperature increases of two to five degrees Celsius by the year 2100," he said, without explaining the source of those numbers. "Last year's models say one to three degrees. Where to next year?"

ICN staff members Zahra Hirji, Paul Horn, Naveena Sadasivam, Sabrina Shankman and Alexander Wood also contributed to this report.

"There is unanimous agreement in the scientific community that a temperature increase of this magnitude would bring about significant changes in the earth's climate, including rainfall distribution and alterations in the biosphere."

Roger Cohen
Exxon Sciences Lab Director
1982

"A major frustration to many is the all-too-apparent bias of IPCC to downplay the significance of scientific uncertainty and gaps."

Brian Flannery
Exxon Position Paper
2002

4. EXXON'S BUSINESS AMBITION COLLIDED WITH CLIMATE CHANGE UNDER A DISTANT SEA

Throughout the 1980s, the company struggled to solve the carbon problem of one of the biggest gas fields in the world out of concern for climate impacts.

By Neela Banerjee and Lisa Song

Oct. 8, 2015

In 1980, as Exxon Corp. set out to develop one of the world's largest deposits of natural gas, it found itself facing an unfamiliar risk: the project would emit immense amounts of carbon dioxide, adding to the looming threat of climate change.

The problem cropped up shortly after Exxon signed a contract with the Indonesian state oil company to exploit the Natuna gas field in the South China Sea—big enough to supply the blossoming markets of Japan, Taiwan and Korea with liquefied natural gas into the 21st century.

Assessing the environmental impacts, Exxon Research and Engineering quickly identified Natuna's greenhouse gas problem. The reservoir was contaminated with much more carbon dioxide than normal. It would have to be disposed of somehow—and simply venting it into the air could have serious consequences, Exxon's experts warned.

Exxon's dawning realization that carbon dioxide and the greenhouse effect posed a danger to the world collided with the company's fossil fuel ambitions.

"They were being farsighted," recalled John L. Woodward, who wrote an internal report in 1981 on Natuna's climate implications.

"They weren't sure when CO_2 controls would be required and how it would affect the economics of the project."

Since 1978, long before the general public grew aware of the climate crisis, Exxon had worked at the cutting edge of emerging climate science. At first, Exxon's internal studies had described climate change as an important but somewhat distant problem. Now, sooner than expected, climate considerations were affecting strategic business decisions. Natuna was one example; another was Exxon's proposed leap into synthetic fuels.

Releasing Natuna's carbon pollution would make it "the world's largest point source emitter of CO_2 and raises concern for the possible incremental impact of Natuna on the CO_2 greenhouse problem," declared an October 1984 report from Exxon's top climate modeler, Brian Flannery, and his boss Andrew Callegari.

Documents and other evidence uncovered by InsideClimate News also show that Exxon calculated that Natuna's emissions would have twice the climate impact of coal. The company spent years researching possible remedies, but found them all too costly or ineffective, ICN's eight-month investigation found.

Exxon managers saw the problem as both technically vexing and environmentally fraught. Not only was there carbon dioxide to be dealt with, it was mixed with toxic, flammable hydrogen sulfide, a contributor to acid rain.

"I think we generally agree that we are seeking a method of disposing of the off gases in a manner which will minimize the risk of environmental damage," wrote Exxon's manager of environmental affairs Alvin M. Natkin in an October 1983 letter to Natuna project executive Richard L. Preston. "We must also have the data which will be convincing not only to ourselves but also to the international environmental community that the method selected is environmentally sound."

The company consulted with leading scientists, including NASA's pioneering expert James E. Hansen, to understand the effect on atmospheric CO_2 concentrations if the gas from Natuna were released. It sent staff to facilities at Dalhousie University in Halifax, Canada to simulate the diffusion of the gas into ocean water. Over the years, Exxon scientists developed mathematical models to assess the options.

Because the project was so complex and expensive, the Natuna staff presented regular updates, including details of the CO_2 issue, to Exxon's board of directors, whose members were drawn almost entirely from the company's upper management.

Some Exxon directors accepted the emerging climate consensus. Others were less sure of the science, but agreed that as popular attention to global warming mounted, releasing Natuna's greenhouse gases into the air could turn into a public relations debacle, former employees said.

Either way, directors repeatedly told project staff Natuna could not proceed unless the CO_2 was handled in a cost-effective way that did not harm the atmosphere.

"Their concerns kept getting stronger," said a former employee with knowledge of the project, who asked for anonymity because the issue remains sensitive even years later. "Their attitude went from, 'Maybe we have to remove the CO_2,' to, as the years went by, their saying, 'This project cannot go ahead unless we remove the CO_2.'"

In 1984, Lee Raymond joined Exxon's board of directors. A senior vice president, Raymond's responsibilities included overseeing Exxon Research and Engineering, which conducted the Natuna studies. In the summer of 1985, ER&E prepared documents for Raymond about a study that examined disposing Natuna's CO_2 into the ocean, an Exxon memo shows.

Eventually, Raymond would rise to become chairman and chief executive, and to lead a public campaign discrediting the scientific consensus on climate change and fighting measures to control greenhouse gas emissions.

In the meantime Exxon, now known as ExxonMobil, appears to have kept its years of climate-related deliberations about Natuna mostly to itself. Exxon only began to disclose climate risks to its shareholders years after it first weighed Natuna's risks, federal filings show.

ExxonMobil declined to answer specific questions for this article. In July, when ICN questioned him for an earlier article about Natuna, spokesman Richard Keil said, "It is company policy not to comment on potential commercial operations."

THE CARBON FOOTPRINT

First discovered by the Italian oil company Agip in the early 1970s, the Natuna gas field lies about 700 miles north of Jakarta and holds about 46 trillion cubic feet of recoverable methane, or natural gas. But the undersea formation also contains 154 trillion cubic feet of other gases, mostly CO_2.

To liquefy Natuna's methane for shipping, it must be supercooled. At those low temperatures, the carbon dioxide would freeze into dry ice and clog equipment, so it had to be removed. The question was where to put it.

The Indonesian government and the state-run oil company had no issue with releasing the CO_2 into the air, former Exxon staff said. But awareness of carbon dioxide's impact on global temperatures had been seeping through Exxon, from its rank-and-file engineers to its board of directors.

"Within Exxon in those days, there were probably two to three believers in global warming for every denier or those who emphasized the uncertainty," said another former Exxon Research executive, who asked not to be identified for fear of reprisal.

Among the key people searching for a solution was Gilbert Gervasi, the Natuna project manager, who worked in Houston under executive Richard Preston for Esso Eastern, the unit that oversaw projects in East Asia. Gervasi spearheaded the effort from the early to mid-1980s to figure out how big Natuna's carbon footprint would be and what to do about it.

In a Feb. 3, 1981 letter to Gene Northington at Research and Engineering, Gervasi challenged a "rough calculation" that Northington had made of the CO_2 emissions from producing Natuna's gas and burning it as fuel. Northington's math showed Natuna's total CO_2 emissions would be "no higher than what would be emitted by burning" an equivalent amount of coal, Gervasi wrote.

After conducting what he described as "more rigorous" calculations, Gervasi concluded "that the total release of CO_2 from producing Natuna gas and burning of the LNG manufactured from the gas would be almost twice that emitted by burning an equivalent amount of coal."

Six months later, Research and Engineering sent Gervasi a report, entitled "Possible Climate Modification Effects of Releasing Carbon Dioxide to the Atmosphere from the Natuna LNG Project." It commissioned assessments of Natuna by seven eminent atmospheric scientists, including the climatologists Helmut Landsberg of University of Maryland and NASA's Hansen.

The report, written by John Woodward, a high level engineer at Exxon Research, presented a mixed message. Natuna would constitute a "small fraction of worldwide CO_2 budget," it found. But it also found that "emissions are nonetheless substantial by several comparisons."

DISPOSAL OPTIONS

Woodward examined the option of flaring the CO_2 after it had been stripped from the natural gas.

Although not combustible, the CO_2 had to be flared rather than simply vented because it was mixed with hydrogen sulfide, which is often burned to convert it to safer compounds. But flaring would not eliminate Natuna's greenhouse gas emissions.

Next, Woodward looked at releasing the CO_2 into seawater around Natuna, a process known as sparging. The gas from the Natuna well would be piped to a nearby platform where the valuable methane would be separated from the waste CO_2 and the toxic hydrogen sulfide. Those unwanted gases, in turn, would then be sent from the platform to a pipe about 300 feet below on the ocean floor. The pipe would be arranged in a circle 6 miles in diameter and the gas would be bubbled out of perforations every six to 10 feet, like aerating an aquarium.

Woodward said that in 1982 he visited the oceanography department at Dalhousie University in Nova Scotia to use their equipment to collect data for sparging models. Dalhousie had a tank about 40 feet high and 10 feet wide, filled with ocean water. Researchers released CO_2 at the bottom of the tank, and Woodward measured the size and quantity of the bubbles at various depths as they rose to the surface to understand how the gas dissipated.

In the end, the hydrogen sulfide released with the CO_2 stymied the sparging idea, Woodward said. Exxon worried that a toxic plume might kill fish and result in bad press.

BACK TO SQUARE ONE

The Natuna project staff and Research and Engineering specialists probed for answers through the 1980s, sometimes revisiting the approaches that Woodward had examined.

In October 1983, Gervasi sent a letter and background paper on Natuna to about a dozen staff and executives from different branches of the corporation to develop "a study program which over the next 1-2 years will put Exxon in a position to reach a final decision on the environmental aspects of the project."

The background paper laid out options to dispose of the CO_2, none of them optimal. Releasing the waste gases into the air remained the simplest, cheapest method. "However, this raises environmental questions concerning the 'greenhouse' effect of the CO_2," the paper said.

Gervasi's paper said the only effective way to dispose of carbon dioxide and hydrogen sulfide without harming the atmosphere or ocean would involve injecting the gases underground into the Natuna formation itself or a nearby reservoir. But that option appeared prohibitively expensive.

Thwarted by cost or environmental impact, Exxon returned to mathematical models over the next two years to home in on a suitable approach.

By February 1984, Exxon Research began modelling once more the feasibility of sparging.

The scientists found that the ocean would release the CO_2 into the atmosphere, probably in 10 years or sooner. Further, increased CO_2 would raise the acidity of the ocean water, damaging the local environment. "Our conclusion is that atmospheric discharge is preferable to seawater sparging," Flannery and others concluded.

Study after study returned Exxon back to square one with Natuna: it held the rights to an enormously promising field but was unable to develop it because it was unwilling to pump so much CO_2 into the air.

The scientists' conclusions were reflected in papers prepared for a 1985 meeting with Lee Raymond on Exxon Research's activities.

Their synopsis said: "We modeled the sub-sea disposal of CO_2 in the shallow basin near the Natuna site and found that retention in the sea is only about a decade, as opposed to 1000 years if the CO_2 is disposed in the deep ocean. We recommend that the sub-sea sparging of CO_2 not be implemented since it offers little advantage over direct atmospheric release."

By the late 1980s, Exxon started to explore pumping the CO_2 back into the Natuna formation, the safest option but probably the priciest.

The company found a cost-effective method to dispose of half of Natuna's CO_2 underground, but calculated that the rest of the CO_2 would still be the equivalent of half of Canada's annual greenhouse gas emissions, said Roger Witherspoon, a former Program Officer in Corporate Contributions in the Public Affairs department.

Company officials asked Witherspoon to find a way to plant 100,000 trees annually to offset Natuna's remaining CO_2 emissions. The total acreage would eventually equal the size of Connecticut, Witherspoon said.

As Witherspoon researched the options starting around 1993, Exxon had embarked on a public campaign casting doubt on climate science as a basis for strong policy actions. Internally, the attitude was different.

"It was that greenhouse gas buildup could pose a threat to our business," said Witherspoon, a longtime journalist who worked at Exxon's Texas headquarters from 1990 to 1995. "You didn't want climate change caused by oil and gas. So the responsible thing to do was offset any greenhouse gases you were putting into the atmosphere."

Witherspoon said Exxon started his tree planting plan, but he does not know how long it lasted.

Exxon continued to investigate possibilities for responsibly disposing of Natuna's CO_2. The project remains dormant, but Exxon never gave up. After an on-and-off relationship with Indonesia, the company still holds the license, which is up for renewal next summer.

"It is now clear that for a number of years, both Bush administration political appointees and a network of organizations funded by the world's largest private energy company, ExxonMobil, have sought to distort, manipulate, and suppress climate science, so as to confuse the American public about the reality and urgency of the global warming problem, and thus forestall a strong policy response."

Dr. James J. McCarthy
American Association for the
Advancement of Science
2007

"ExxonMobil has always advocated for good public policy that is based on sound science. We will continue to do that despite criticism from those who make unsupported and inaccurate claims about our company."

Ken Cohen
Exxon VP of Public &
Government Affairs
2015

5. HIGHLIGHTING THE ALLURE OF SYNFUELS, EXXON PLAYED DOWN THE CLIMATE RISKS

In the 1980s, Exxon lobbied to replace scarce oil with synthetic fossil fuels, but it glossed over the high carbon footprint associated with synfuels.

By John H. Cushman Jr.

Oct. 8, 2015

Early in the 1980s, the lingering fear of oil scarcity and the emerging threat of climate change were beginning to intersect. And at that junction stood Exxon Corp., working out its strategy for survival in the uncertain 21st century.

At the time, Exxon believed oil supplies could not keep up with demand, so it put its weight behind a crusade to develop synthetic fossil fuels as a costly and carbon intensive, but potentially profitable alternative. It could liquefy the vast deposits of coal, oil shale and tar sands that were readily available in North America. This would be the new black gold, supplying as much as a third of the energy the United States would use in the early 21st century, company executives estimated.

"These resources are adequate to support a 15 million barrel a day industry for 175 years," said Randall Meyer, a senior vice president, in a 1981 speech before the U.S. Chamber of Commerce.

By then, however, researchers at Exxon were well aware of the looming problem of climate change. Years earlier, one climate researcher at the company, Henry Shaw, had called management's attention to a key conclusion of a landmark National Academy of Sciences report: global warming caused by carbon dioxide emissions, not a scarcity of supply, would likely set the ultimate limit on the use of fossil fuels.

Yet in his speech, Meyer said nothing about the carbon footprint of synfuels – even though the company was aware that making and burning them would release much more carbon dioxide into the atmosphere than ordinary oil.

In a 21-page speech, Meyer explained that a national synfuels program would require investing almost $800 billion (in 1980 dollars) over three decades. He said it would create 870,000 jobs. It would, he promised, carry the nation through a long-term transition to "non-depleting and renewable" energy sources.

"Over the past couple of years my associates and I have talked about synthetic fuels as a major national need to a lot of audiences," he noted. "In the federal government, that included the White House and most cabinet members. At the state level, we visited with governors, and a good many senators and congressmen. We have had audiences like GM's and Ford's senior managements, the Business Roundtable, national labor leaders, major media companies, influential academics and many others."

The government did respond, with a costly synfuels program that ultimately folded as oil markets turned from shortage to glut and the technology proved to be unaffordable. Congress withdrew funding from the United States Synfuels Corporation, and most forms of synfuels production never grew to global significance.

One important remnant that survived was the industry's foray into tar sands oil, especially in Canada, where Exxon would become a major player – and where the carbon dioxide problem still plagues the industry after more than three decades. Recent research finds that substantial growth in tar sands production is incompatible with keeping CO_2 emissions below the internationally accepted target of 2 degrees C.

But in the early days of synfuels, as Exxon defended them as a costly but plausible solution to oil scarcity, it sidestepped the carbon problem. In the text of a speech by Exxon chief executive Clifton Garvin before a particularly skeptical audience, the Environmental Defense Fund, in April 1981, global warming was never mentioned among the environmental risks that he said the industry would be "held primarily responsible for solving."

Nor, it appears, did Exxon elaborate on the link between synfuels and global warming in annual reports to shareholders filed with regulatory agencies in those early days, when synfuels remained at the heart of the company's long term ambitions.

Yet all along, there had been a bubbling concern among researchers, including some inside Exxon, about the carbon implications of synfuels.

Company documents discovered during an eight-month investigation by

InsideClimate News show that Exxon Research & Engineering estimated that producing and burning oil shales would release 1.4 to 3 times more carbon dioxide than conventional oil, and would accelerate the doubling of greenhouse gases in the atmosphere by about five years. The company knew that a doubling would risk about 3 degrees Celsius of warming, or 5.4 degrees Fahrenheit.

The company was tracking the research closely. When two U.S. Geological Survey scientists estimated in Science magazine in 1979 that the carbon footprint from synfuels might be three to five times more than conventional fuels, ER&E climate researcher Henry Shaw wrote in a memo that the upper range "may alarm the public unjustifiably."

As early as November, 1979, Shaw had told Harold Weinberg in a memo on atmospheric research that environmental groups "have already attempted to curb the budding synfuels industry because it could accelerate the buildup of CO_2 in the atmosphere." He warned Exxon not to be caught off guard, the way the aviation industry had been surprised by the threat to supersonic airplane development when the ozone hole was discovered.

In 1980, after attending a federal advisory committee meeting, Shaw explained why he didn't think the carbon dioxide problem would block work on synfuels any time soon.

"I attended the last meeting of this committee on January 17 and 18, 1980, and found such a vast diversity of interests and backgrounds that I believe no imminent action is possible," he wrote in a memo.

"For example, some environmentalists suggested that all development of synthetic fuels be terminated until sufficient information becomes available to permit adequate strategic decisions to be made. The industrial representation, on the other hand, indicated that the build up of CO_2 in the atmosphere was not necessarily anthropogenic, and is of little consequence for the next century."

But Shaw also circulated a clipping from The New York Times in August 1981, under the headline "Synthetic Fuels Called a Peril to the Atmosphere."

In the article, the Associated Press quoted an economist named Lester Lave as testifying before Congress that "if we take CO_2 seriously, we would change drastically the energy policy we are pursuing."

As in so many other realms of its research, Exxon studied a potential future of synthetic fuels while recognizing that carbon dioxide could be a powerful factor in its business decisions for decades to come.

"We are very pleased with Exxon's research intentions related to the CO_2 question. This represents very responsible action, which we hope will serve as a model for research contributions from the corporate sector. This is truly a national and international service."

David Slade
US Department of Energy
2002

"To call ExxonMobil's position out of the mainstream is thus a gross understatement. To be in opposition to the key scientific findings is rather appalling for such an established and scientific organization."

Michael MacCracken
US Global Change Research
Program
2002

6. EXXON SOWED DOUBT ABOUT CLIMATE SCIENCE FOR DECADES BY STRESSING UNCERTAINTY

Collaborating with the Bush-Cheney White House, Exxon turned ordinary scientific uncertainties into weapons of mass confusion.

By David Hasemyer and John H. Cushman Jr.

Oct. 22, 2015

As he wrapped up nine years as the federal government's chief scientist for global warming research, Michael MacCracken lashed out at ExxonMobil for opposing the advance of climate science.

His own great-grandfather, he told the Exxon board, had been John D. Rockefeller's legal counsel a century earlier. "What I rather imagine he would say is that you are on the wrong side of history, and you need to find a way to change your position," he wrote.

Addressed to chairman Lee Raymond on the letterhead of the United States Global Change Research Program, his September 2002 letter was not just forceful, but unusually personal.

No wonder: in the opening days of the oil-friendly Bush-Cheney administration, Exxon's chief lobbyist had written the new head of the White House environmental council demanding that MacCracken be fired for "political and scientific bias."

Exxon was also attacking other officials in the U.S. government and at the UN's Intergovernmental Panel on Climate Change (IPCC), MacCracken wrote, interfering with their work behind the scenes and distorting it in public.

Exxon wanted scientists who disputed the mainstream science on climate change to oversee Washington's work with the IPCC, the authoritative body that defines the scientific consensus on global warming, documents written by an Exxon lobbyist and one of its scientists show. The company persuaded the White House to block the reappointment of the IPCC chairman, a World Bank scientist. Exxon's top climate researcher, Brian Flannery, was pushing the White House for a wholesale revision of federal climate science. The company wanted a new strategy to focus on the uncertainties.

"To call ExxonMobil's position out of the mainstream is thus a gross understatement," MacCracken wrote. "To be in opposition to the key scientific findings is rather appalling for such an established and scientific organization."

MacCracken had a long history of collaboration with Exxon researchers. He knew that during the 1970s and 1980s, well before the general public understood the risks of global warming, the company's researchers had worked at the cutting edge of climate change science. He had edited and even co-authored some of their reports. So he found it galling that Exxon was now leading a concerted effort to sow confusion about fossil fuels, carbon dioxide and the greenhouse effect.

Exxon had turned a colleague into its enemy.

It was a vivid example of Exxon's undermining of mainstream science and embrace of denial and misinformation, which became most pronounced after President George W. Bush took office. The campaign climaxed when Bush pulled out of the Kyoto Protocol in 2001. Taking the U.S. out of the international climate change treaty was Exxon's key goal, and the reason for its persistent emphasis on the uncertainty of climate science.

This in-depth series by InsideClimate News has explored Exxon's early engagement with climate research more than 35 years ago – and its subsequent use of scientific uncertainty as a shield against forceful action on global warming. The series is based on Exxon documents, interviews, and other evidence from an eight-month investigation.

"What happened was an incredible disconnect in people trained in physical science and engineering," recalled Martin Hoffert, a New York University professor who collaborated with Exxon's team as its early computer modeling confirmed the emerging scientific consensus on global warming. "It's an untold story of how we got to the point where climate change has become a threat to the world."

THE UNCERTAINTY AGENDA

As the Bush-Cheney administration arrived in the White House in 2001, ExxonMobil (NYSE: XOM) now had partners for a climate uncertainty strategy.

Just weeks after Bush was sworn in, Exxon's top lobbyist Randy Randol sent the White House a memo complaining that "Clinton/Gore carry-overs with aggressive agendas" were still playing a role at the IPCC as it prepared its next assessment of the climate science consensus.

MacCracken and three colleagues should be replaced, or at least kept out of "any decisional activities," he wrote. Meanwhile, U.S. input to the IPCC should be delayed.

Further, two scientists highly critical of the prevailing consensus should be enlisted: John Christy of the University of Alabama should take the science lead and Richard Lindzen of MIT should review U.S. submissions to the IPCC.

Exxon had been circulating a proposal to fundamentally overhaul MacCracken's global change research program, by emphasizing the uncertainties of climate science.

The timing was not coincidental because the administration, as required by law, was about to lay out a new federal climate research strategy. Exxon and its allies wanted the work done during the Clinton-Gore years to be marginalized.

In March 2002, Flannery, Exxon's science strategy and programs manager, contacted John H. Marburger, the president's incoming assistant for science and technology, to pitch the company's favored approach of emphasizing the uncertainty. Earlier discussions, he asserted, "have not sought to place the uncertainty in the context of why it is important to public policy."

Exxon's position paper, attached to his letter, took a dig at the work of the IPCC.

"A major frustration to many is the all-too-apparent bias of IPCC to downplay the significance of scientific uncertainty and gaps," the memo said.

A SEAT AT THE TABLE

Exxon had not always been so at odds with the prevailing science.
Since the late 1970s, Exxon scientists had been telling top

41

executives that the most likely cause of climate change was carbon pollution from the combustion of fossil fuels, and that it was important to get a grip on the problem quickly. Exxon Research & Engineering had launched innovative ocean research from aboard the company's biggest supertanker, the Esso Atlantic. ER&E's modeling experts, by the early 1980s, had confirmed the consensus among outside scientists about the climate's sensitivity to carbon dioxide.

"The facts are that we identified the potential risks of climate change and have taken the issue very seriously," said Ken Cohen, Exxon's vice president of public and government affairs, in a press release on October 21 addressing the ICN reports. "We embarked on decades of research in collaboration with many parties."

Exxon has declined to answer specific questions from InsideClimate News.

A 1980 memo proposed an ambitious public-relations plan aimed at "achieving national recognition of our CO_2 Greenhouse research program."

"It is significant to Exxon since future public decisions aimed at controlling the build-up of atmospheric CO_2 could impose limits on fossil fuel combustion," said the memo. "It is significant to all humanity since, although the CO_2 Greenhouse Effect is not today widely perceived as a threat, the popular media are giving increased attention to doom-saying theories about dramatic climate changes and melting polar icecaps."

Most of all, Exxon wanted a seat at the policy-making table, and the credibility of its research had earned that. In 1979, David Slade, manager of carbon dioxide research at the Energy Department, called it "a model for research contributions from the corporate sector."

Sen. Gary Hart, a Colorado Democrat, invited Henry Shaw, an early Exxon scientist, to join the policy deliberations. He was the only industry representative invited to an October 1980 conference of the National Commission on Air Quality, newly set up by Congress, to discuss "whether potential consequences of increased carbon dioxide levels warrant development of policies to mitigate adverse effects."

Shaw's bosses agreed that he should attend, "both to be informed as to what actions or proposals that result and to bring objective thinking and information to the meeting," Harold Weinberg, Shaw's boss in Exxon Research and Engineering, wrote in a memo. But first, he said, Shaw needed to be briefed by public affairs executives "on possible hidden agenda and individual biases of which we may not already be aware."

When Shaw gave feedback to the commission in December, he noted the uncertainties about carbon dioxide and climate change. At the same time, he wrote that it was "important" to place CO_2 on the nation's public policy agenda, as the commission was recommending, and supported the panel's suggestion that it was "timely to consider ways of reducing

CO_2 emissions now."

He also backed a recommendation that the U.S. "seek to develop discussions on national and international policies."

In late spring of 1981, Flannery was one of the few industry representatives at a large gathering of accomplished scientists at Harper's Ferry, W. Va., for a Department of Energy "Workshop on First Detection of Carbon Dioxide Effects." He sat on a panel with NASA's James Hansen, who was about to publish a landmark study in Science magazine warning of significant warming even if controls were placed on carbon emissions.

The workshop's proceedings would declare that "scientists are agreed" that carbon dioxide was building up in the atmosphere, that the effects "are well known" and "will bring about an increase in the mean global temperature," and that it is "commonly accepted" that warming "will affect the biosphere through a change in climate."

Working with Hoffert, Flannery wrote a highly technical 50-page chapter to a 1985 Energy Department report. Their modeling projected up to 6 degrees Celsius of warming by the end of the 21st century unless emissions of greenhouse gases were curtailed.

The influential government report said the models provided a "firm basis" for this kind of projection, and that "we are already committed to some of this warming as a result of emissions over the last several decades."

The Harper's Ferry conference was chaired by MacCracken; he also edited the warming report. He recalled recently that "the underlying push was for a level of understanding that was convincing enough to let policymakers become aware of what the issue was that society faced."

As Hoffert put it in a recent interview, in those days at Exxon "there were no divisions, no agendas. We were coming together as scientists to address issues of vital importance to the world."

FORK IN THE ROAD

In 1988, James Hansen told Congress that there was now enough warming to declare that the greenhouse effect had arrived. Also that year, the United Nations set up the Intergovernmental Panel on Climate Change.

It was a moment that Exxon's climate experts had been forecasting for a decade: that as warming became unmistakable, governments would move to control it.

Looking backward, one Exxon document from the early 1990s reflects a trail of research into global warming stretching back "long before the issue achieved its current prominence."

An internal compendium of the company's environmental record, on file in the official ExxonMobil historical archives at the University of Texas-Austin, acknowledged the uncertainties that have always faced climate researchers, but it didn't downplay the risks.

"Fossil fuel use dominates as the source of man-made emissions of carbon dioxide," said one section of the encyclopedic review. "Current scientific understanding demonstrates the potential for climate change to produce serious impacts."

"For Exxon and the petroleum industry, potential enhancement of the greenhouse effect and the possibility of adverse climate are of particular and fundamental concern," it said.

DRILLING FOR UNCERTAINTY

The IPCC published its first report in 1990. Despite the scientific gaps, the panel warned that unrestrained emissions from burning fossil fuels would surely warm the planet in the century ahead. The conclusion, the IPCC said after intense deliberations, was "certain." It prescribed deep reductions in greenhouse gas emissions to stave off a crisis in the coming decades.

At this crucial juncture, Exxon pivoted toward uncertainty and away from the global scientific consensus.

At the IPCC's final session to draft its summary for policymakers, Exxon's Flannery was in the room as an observer. He took the microphone to challenge both the certainty and the remedy. None of the other scientists agreed with Flannery, and the IPCC brushed off Exxon's advice to water down the report, according to Jeremy Leggett's eyewitness account in his book, *The Carbon War*.

At a conference in June 1991, MacCracken joined a panel chaired by Flannery to work together on a climate change project involving geo-engineering.

The contact, according to MacCracken, led to an unexpected solicitation from the oil lobby in Washington. Will Ollison, a science adviser at the American Petroleum Institute, in a fax marked urgent, asked MacCracken, then at the Lawrence Livermore National Laboratory, to write a paper highlighting the scientific uncertainties surrounding global warming.

The API, where Exxon held enormous sway, wanted him to write up the complex nuances in plain English – with an emphasis on the unknown, not the known.

Ollison said the IPCC's 1990 report "may not have adequately addressed alternative views."

"A review of these alternative projections would be useful in illustrating the uncertainties inherent in the 'consensus' views expressed in the IPCC report," Ollison wrote.

MacCracken rejected the task as "fruitless."

"I would caution you about too readily accepting whatever the naysayers put forth as a means of achieving balance," MacCracken wrote back.

Flannery, for his part, continued to emphasize uncertainty. And so did Exxon's new chairman and chief executive, Lee Raymond, who spoke of it repeatedly in public.

"Currently, the scientific evidence is inconclusive as to whether human activities are having a significant effect on the global climate," Raymond claimed in a speech delivered in 1996 to the Economic Club of Detroit.

"Many people, politicians and the public alike, believe that global warming is a rock-solid certainty," he said the next year in a speech in Beijing. "But it's not."

Addressing the World Petroleum Congress, which was meeting just before the conclusion of the Kyoto Protocol negotiations, Raymond even disputed that the planet was warming at all. "The earth is cooler today than it was 20 years ago," he said.

That was false. Authoritative climate agencies declared 1997 the warmest year ever measured. Decade by decade, the warming has continued, in line with the climate models.

But Raymond, turning his back on Exxon researchers and their state-of-the-art work, mocked those climate models.

"1990's models were predicting temperature increases of two to five degrees Celsius by the year 2100. Last year's models say one to three degrees. Where to next year?"

"It is highly unlikely," he said, "that the temperature in the middle of the next century will be significantly affected whether policies are enacted now or 20 years from now."

THE DOUBT INDUSTRY

Exxon and its allies had been working hard to spread this dilatory message.

First, they set up the Global Climate Coalition (GCC), a lobbying partnership of leading oil and automobile companies dedicated to defeating controls on carbon pollution.

"As major corporations with a high level of internal scientific and technical expertise, they were aware of and in a position to understand the available scientific data," recounts an essay on corporate responsibility for climate change published last month in the peer-reviewed journal Climatic

Change.

"From 1989 to 2002, the GCC led an aggressive lobbying and advertising campaign aimed at achieving these goals by sowing doubt about the integrity of the IPCC and the scientific evidence that heat-trapping emissions from burning fossil fuels drive global warming," says the article, by Harvard climate science historian Naomi Oreskes and two co-authors.

Then, in 1998 Exxon also helped create the Global Climate Science Team, an effort involving Randy Randol, the company's top lobbyist, and Joe Walker, a public relations representative for API.

Their memo, leaked to The New York Times, asserted that it is "not known for sure whether (a) climate change actually is occurring, or (b) if it is, whether humans really have any influence on it." Opponents of the Kyoto treaty, it complained, "have done little to build a case against precipitous action on climate change based on the scientific uncertainty."

The memo declared: "Victory will be achieved when average citizens 'understand' (recognize) uncertainties in climate science," and when "recognition of uncertainty becomes part of the 'conventional wisdom.'"

Exxon wholeheartedly embraced that theme. For example, an advertisement called "Unsettled Science" that ran in major papers in the spring of 2000, prompted one scientist to complain that it had distorted his work by suggesting it supported the notion that global warming was just a natural cycle. "It's a shame," Lloyd Keigwin later told the Wall Street Journal. "The implication is that these data show that we don't need to worry about global warming."

Another ad, one of a series placed in The New York Times, cast aspersions on scientists who "believe they can predict changes in climate decades from now."

Then, in the heat of the 2000 presidential race between climate champion Al Gore and erstwhile oilman George W. Bush, Exxon placed an ad in the Washington Post accusing MacCracken's office of putting the "political cart before a scientific horse."

BLOWING THE WHISTLE

The collaboration between Exxon, its surrogates, and the Bush administration to emphasize uncertainty and stave off action came to light in 2005. A whistleblower named Rick Piltz disclosed that Philip Cooney, an oil lobbyist who had become chief of staff at the White House environmental council, had been heavily editing the work of government researchers. Cooney resigned, and was hired by Exxon.

But the clashes continued between the scientific establishment and

Exxon's purveyors of uncertainty.

The Royal Society of the United Kingdom, for centuries a renowned arbiter of science, harshly criticized Exxon in 2006 for publishing "very misleading" statements about the IPCC's Third Assessment Report. The IPCC found that most of the observed warming of the planet in the late 20th century was probably caused by humans.

The Society's communications manager Bob Ward reminded Exxon pointedly that one of its own scientists had contributed to the IPCC chapter in question.

The Royal Society said it had no problem with Exxon funding scientific research, but "we do have concerns about ExxonMobil's funding of lobby groups that seek to misrepresent the scientific evidence relating to climate change."

Ward said Exxon was funding at least 39 organizations "featuring information on their websites that misrepresented the science on climate change, by outright denial of the evidence that greenhouse gases are driving climate change, or by overstating the amount and significance of uncertainty in knowledge."

Exxon's uncertainty campaign was detailed in three exhaustive reports published in 2007 by the Union of Concerned Scientists and the Government Accountability Project.

At a Congressional hearing in 2007, Harvard scientist James McCarthy, who was a member of the UCS board and the newly elected president of the American Association for the Advancement of Science, declared: "The Bush administration and a network of Exxon-funded, ExxonMobil funded organizations have sought to distort, manipulate and suppress climate science so as to confuse the American public about the urgency of the global warming problem, and thus, forestall a strong policy response."

To this day, top Exxon officials sometimes argue that models are no basis for policy.

While Rex Tillerson, the current chairman, doesn't echo Lee Raymond's science denial in his formal speeches, he sometimes backslides when speaking off the cuff.

At Exxon's annual meeting in 2015, Tillerson said it would be best to wait for more solid science before acting on climate change. "What if everything we do, it turns out our models are lousy, and we don't get the effects we predict?" he asked.

And in its formal annual energy forecasts, as well as in its latest report on the implications of its carbon footprint, Exxon adopts business-as-usual assumptions. It deflects the question of how much carbon will build up in the world's atmosphere over the next few decades, or how much the planet will warm as a result.

"As part of our energy outlook process, we do not project overall atmospheric GHG [greenhouse gas] concentration, nor do we model global average temperature impacts," both reports say.

In footnotes, Exxon offers this excuse: "These would require data inputs that are well beyond our company's ability to reasonably measure or verify."

ICN staff members Neela Banerjee, Lisa Song, Zahra Hirji, and Paul Horn also contributed to this report.

7. EXXON MADE DEEP CUTS IN CLIMATE RESEARCH BUDGET IN THE 1980S

The cuts ushered in a five-year hiatus in peer-reviewed publication by its scientists and the era when the company first embraced disinformation.

By John H. Cushman Jr.

Nov. 25, 2015

Internal Exxon Corporation budget documents from the 1980s show that the oil giant sharply curtailed its ambitious program of innovative climate research in those years, chopping well over half from its annual budget for internal investigations into how carbon dioxide emissions from fossil fuels would affect the planet.

Facing a budget crunch and sensing that any government efforts to clamp down on carbon pollution were a long way off, Exxon terminated two especially innovative experiments. One involved oceanic observations during voyages of the Esso Atlantic, a supertanker. The other proposed to test vintage French wines for tell-tale traces of carbon dioxide from fossil fuels or other sources.

And then, in the late 1980s, Exxon ramped up a decades-long public relations campaign to sow uncertainty about the increasing scientific evidence for urgent action on climate change.

Exxon's pivoting from the cutting edge of early climate change science to the forefront of climate denial was described in a six-part series published by InsideClimate News beginning in September, based largely on primary sources including Exxon's own internal documents. Similar findings were reached independently by a team based at the Columbia

Journalism School in partnership with the Los Angeles Times.

Exxon spokesman Ken Cohen has questioned ICN's reporting that the company "curtailed" its research program after a few years of unusually advanced experiments and modeling work in the 1980s.

But several documents uncovered by ICN show that the budget cuts during the 1980s were steep and sudden. The cuts reversed the course that the company followed in the late 1970s, when top company scientists warned Exxon's management for the first time of the risks of climate change, and launched internal research programs unparalleled among its oil industry peers.

ICN provided an Exxon spokesman copies of the documents being published today and requested any additional information about climate research spending during the 1980s, the period closely examined in ICN's series, "Exxon: The Road Not Taken." The spokesman, Alan Jeffers, declined to provide any additional budget numbers.

One of the documents, a June 18, 1982 memo to Harold Weinberg, a top research official, informed him that the year's budget for research into the looming CO2 problem was to be cut from $900,000 to $385,000 immediately, and to just $150,000 the following year, an 83 percent cut.

"We feel this rate of expenditure should be sufficient to fulfill the Corporation's needs in the CO2 greenhouse field," said the memo, written by A.M. Natkin, environmental affairs coordinator in the corporate science and technology department.

"These funds are intended to support a resident source of scientific expertise on all phases and aspects of the CO2 Greenhouse effect," he wrote. "It is important for the corporation to stay abreast of developments in order to assess the impact of new scientific discoveries and to respond to various inquiries."

He said that $150,000 a year "should be sufficient to do this."

Exxon's annual research and development budget at the time was more than $600 million, according to a speech by Exxon Research & Engineering chief Ed David at a 1981 Exxon R&D symposium in San Francisco. The company's exploration and capital budgets amounted to $11 billion.

The Natkin memo augured the dismantling of the crown jewel of Exxon's early research on climate change: a seagoing field experiment into the ocean's absorption of carbon dioxide emissions from the burning of fossil fuels. Once envisioned as an expanding, multiyear effort, it was terminated in 1982, another memo confirmed.

Another innovative proposal to test the carbon dioxide in old vintages of fine French wines also fell by the wayside.

An additional internal document, this one an October 4, 1985 update presented by Brian Flannery, Exxon's top climate researcher, showed that Exxon's budget for CO2 research in 1985 and 1986 would be no more than

$250,000 each year.

That was to cover professional work by Exxon employees, payments to consultants or contractors for research, travel and miscellaneous expenses, and payments to the Lamont-Doherty Earth Observatory of Columbia University, which was a partner in the tanker project and other early Exxon work.

Exxon's documents show not only that the research was curtailed, but why.

The idea to cut back the research program first surfaced in a January 1981 "scoping study." That was a type of internal Exxon planning document meant to be the "initial phase in the development of comprehensive plans for high-impact programs," a cover sheet explained.

"Our recommendation is that comprehensive program plan development not be undertaken for the atmospheric CO2 area," said the cover sheet.

After all, said the 16-page scoping study, "There is no near term threat of legislation to control CO2. One reason for this is that it has not yet been proven that the increases in atmospheric CO2 constitute a serious problem that requires immediate action."

The scoping study, a 16-page document, was published by ICN as part of the first installment of its six-part investigative series.

"The increasing level of atmospheric CO2 is causing considerable concern due to potential climate effects," the document said. Exxon Research & Engineering, it noted, "has been actively conducting research on certain aspects of the issue for approximately two years. This report addresses the question of whether a comprehensive research plan with greater breadth for ER&E than the current plan should be developed."

The answer to that question was, in short, no. The work "if successful, will likely provide recognition for Exxon for making important technical contributions to this global environmental issue," according to the document.

However, "an expanded R&D program does not appear to offer significantly increased benefits," the document went on. "It would require skills which are in limited supply, and would require additional funds on the part of Exxon since Government funding appears unlikely."

In the mid-1980s the company wrapped up publication of a burst of modeling efforts undertaken during the heyday of its early research–including three important peer-reviewed studies, all described in the ICN series. Those studies by Exxon scientists and consultants, one of them published by the federal government and two by academic journals, confirmed the emerging consensus regarding the planet's sensitivity to increased concentrations of carbon dioxide in the atmosphere.

Then Exxon's published research hit a five-year hiatus, as shown in Exxon's own list of more than 50 peer-reviewed climate studies its employees have worked on.

From 1986 to 1990, Exxon went without publishing any peer-reviewed scientific research into the problem, just as it was becoming a hot topic of political debate.

In 1988, 1989 and 1990, Exxon sharply escalated its well-documented efforts to emphasize the scientific uncertainty surrounding climate change, a campaign of misinformation that would last for decades.

Exxon asserts that it has been doing important scientific research continuously since the 1970s. It frequently mentions its financial support for work done by programs at the Massachusetts Institute of Technology. (Exxon's support for work at Stanford University, more costly and more geared to developing technologies as opposed to understanding climate change itself, began much later.)

Announced in 1993, Exxon's first grant of $1 million to the MIT program was expressly designed to produce assessments "based on realistic representations of the uncertainties of climate science." That phrase occurred both in the press release announcing the grant and, a year later, in the program's first report, entitled "Uncertainty in Climate Change Policy Analysis."

In the light of 20 years of hindsight, that 1994 MIT report's conclusions seem vague and equivocal, providing "no guidance for greenhouse policy."

It said "neither of the extreme positions, to take urgent action now or do nothing awaiting firm evidence, is a constructive response to the climate threat."

"Uncertainty is the essence of the issue," it declared.

8. MORE EXXON DOCUMENTS SHOW HOW MUCH IT KNEW ABOUT CLIMATE 35 YEARS AGO

Documents reveal Exxon's early CO2 position, its global warming forecast from the 1980s, and its involvement with the issue at the highest echelons.

By Neela Banerjee

Dec. 1, 2015

(EDITOR'S NOTE: The documents mentioned in this article, as well as the others in this series, can be accessed at insideclimatenews.org)

In our series, "Exxon: The Road Not Taken," InsideClimate News published several dozen documents that established the arc of Exxon's pioneering yet little-known climate research, which began 40 years ago.

Our reporting team chose them from the thousands of mainly internal company documents that we reviewed in our 10-month investigation.

In addition to the ones we have already published since September—which ExxonMobil has now downloaded from the ICN website and imported to its blog—there are more worth sharing.

Each illuminates a nuance of Exxon's early internal discussions about climate change, from interactions at the highest echelons to presentations for the rank-and-file. The documents reveal the contrast between Exxon's initial public statements about climate change and the company's later efforts to deny the link between fossil fuel use and higher global temperatures.

A selection of previously unpublished memos and reports are included and explained here, as part of ICN's continuing exploration of Exxon's climate documents.

EXXON SENIOR VICE PRESIDENT WEIGHS IN ON THE 'GREENHOUSE PROGRAM' (1980)

A memo from June 9, 1980, indicates that carbon dioxide research was not a project that Exxon's board simply greenlighted. It was an issue so important that at least one senior vice president was paying close attention to the science, and he was interested and versed enough to argue its arcana.

On June 9, 1980, Harold N. Weinberg, a top manager in Exxon Research and Engineering, the hub of the company's carbon dioxide research, sent a note to Richard Werthamer and Henry Shaw with the subject, "Greenhouse Program," the company's CO_2 research initiative. Shaw was the unit's lead climate researcher at the time, Werthamer his boss.

In the note, Weinberg wrote that he gave a presentation at a June 4 meeting about the program and said, "George Piercy questioned me closely on the statement that there is a net CO_2 flux out of the ocean at the upwelling zones."

At the time, Exxon had deployed a state-of-the-art supertanker outfitted with equipment for measuring marine CO_2 concentrations to understand the role the oceans play in the world's carbon cycle. Scientists knew that the oceans had absorbed some of the carbon dioxide released from the increased global consumption of fossil fuels. But Exxon's researchers wanted to understand how exactly CO_2 behaved in the oceans—and whether after trapping the gas, the seas would eventually release it into the atmosphere.

Piercy was a senior vice president at Exxon in 1980, and a member of the board of directors. According to the note, he challenged Weinberg's assertion that global circulation patterns move CO_2 out of the deep oceans to the surface where it escapes into the atmosphere, a process known as "upwelling."

Piercy disagreed, arguing the oceans can hold higher concentrations of CO_2 without releasing it into the air. (As it turns out, Weinberg was right, though overall, the world's oceans act as a global sink, pulling CO2 from the air into the water and helping dampen the effects of climate change.)

Other memos from the early 1980s show that ER&E staff regularly apprised at least one other senior vice president, M.E.J. O'Loughlin, of the latest climate research, too.

EXXON'S LEAD CLIMATE RESEARCHER PRESENTS: THE COMPANY'S POSITION ON THE CO_2 GREENHOUSE EFFECT (1981)

In a May 15, 1981 memo, Exxon estimates a 3-degree Celsius rise in global average temperatures in 100 years, and appears ready to discuss publicly that a time could arrive when the world would have to shift to renewable energy. Exxon thought such a transition could happen in a gradual, "orderly" way.

By 1981, Exxon had already established itself as a leader on the greenhouse effect with many in industry and the government. In early May of that year, Henry Shaw prepared a "brief summary of our current position on the CO_2 Greenhouse effect" for Edward E. David, Jr., president of Exxon Research and Engineering, in case the topic came up at an Exxon symposium in San Francisco where David would be speaking.

Based on documentary evidence, it appears the summary went through several drafts and the final version went to David's office on May 15.

The bullet points that Shaw presented to David start with the idea that "there is sufficient time to study the problem before corrective action is required." Shaw based his caution on estimates that higher global temperatures caused by rising CO_2 would only be felt around the year 2000, and that CO_2 concentrations in the atmosphere would double in about 100 years. Those gaps, Shaw wrote, permit "time for an orderly transition to non-fossil fuel technologies should restrictions on fossil fuel use be deemed necessary."

The document did not raise doubts about the links between fossil fuel use, higher CO_2 concentrations and a warmer planet. Shaw wrote:

• "Atmospheric CO_2 will double in 100 years if fossil fuels grow at 1.4%/ a^2.
• 3°C global average temperature rise and 10°C at poles if CO_2 doubles.
—Major shifts in rainfall/agriculture
—Polar ice may melt"

Eleven other staff and managers at Exxon Research, besides David, were sent the paper with the corporate position on global warming that Shaw had articulated.

By the end of the 1980s, Exxon would publicly pivot away from open consideration of any restrictions on fossil fuel use because of its effect on the atmosphere.

In 1996, when climate research was more certain about the link between fossil fuel combustion and climate change than during the time of Shaw's memo, Exxon's new chairman and chief executive Lee Raymond said in a speech in Detroit: "Currently, the scientific evidence is inconclusive as to whether human activities are having a significant effect on the global climate."

At Exxon's annual meeting in 2015, chairman Rex Tillerson said it would be best to wait for more solid science before acting on climate change. "What if [after] everything we do, it turns out our models are lousy, and we don't get the effects we predict?"

A PRESENTATION ON 'CO$_2$ GREENHOUSE AND CLIMATE ISSUES' (1984)

Exxon began incorporating CO$_2$ estimates into its corporate planning as early as 1981, a March 28, 1984 presentation shows. The company acknowledged the link between fossil fuel use and climate change throughout most of the 1980s.

In 1984, Shaw no longer ran Exxon's CO$_2$ research. He had been moved from that post a few years earlier as the company shifted its focus from the expensive empirical research on the tanker to cheaper, yet still highly significant, climate modeling. By the mid-1980s, Shaw worked on keeping track of emerging independent climate research and apprising top managers.

On March 28, Shaw gave a presentation at an internal Exxon environmental conference in Florham Park, N.J. He showed projections of fossil fuel use through the 21st century and the growth in global carbon dioxide expected from it.

Shaw told his audience that he was regularly asked to prepare estimates for Exxon about CO$_2$ from fossil fuel use. Those estimates used and were integrated into the company's energy projections for the 21st century and circulated within Exxon.

He wrote in the presentation: "As part of CPPD's technology forecasting activities in 1981, I wrote a CO$_2$ greenhouse forecast based on publically available information. Soon thereafter, S&T [Science & Technology] requested an update of the forecast using Exxon fossil fuel projections. This request was followed late in 1981 with a request by CPD [Corporate Planning Department] for assistance in evaluating the potential impact of the CO$_2$ effect in the '2030 Study.' After meeting CPD's specific need, a formal technology forecast update was issued to S&T in the beginning of April 1982. It was subsequently sent for review to the Exxon affiliates."

Exxon's affiliates are the company's various divisions, including exploration and production, refining, international units and shipping.

Then Shaw shared with his audience estimates by Exxon and three other entities—the Environmental Protection Agency, the National Academy of Sciences, and the Massachusetts Institute of Technology—about when CO_2 would double in the atmosphere, what kind of increases could occur in average global temperatures and the effects of such changes on human life.

Exxon estimated that CO_2 would double by 2090, which was later than what the other groups had projected. It estimated that average global temperatures would rise by 1.3 to 3.1 degrees Celsius (2.3 to 5.6 degrees Fahrenheit), which was in the mid-range of the four projections that Shaw shared.

Shaw showed the policy recommendations of the three organizations and Exxon to address climate change. According to him, MIT argued for an "extreme reduction in fossil fuel use," while the others, including Exxon, urged a more cautious approach. But Exxon did not deny the link between fossil fuel use and climate change as it would begin to do just five years later.

ICN reporter Lisa Song contributed to this report.

9. EXXON'S OIL INDUSTRY PEERS KNEW ABOUT CLIMATE DANGERS IN THE 1970S, TOO

Members of an American Petroleum Institute task force on CO2 included scientists from nearly every major oil company, including Exxon, Texaco and Shell.

By Neela Banerjee

Dec. 22, 2015

The American Petroleum Institute together with the nation's largest oil companies ran a task force to monitor and share climate research between 1979 and 1983, indicating that the oil industry, not just Exxon alone, was aware of its possible impact on the world's climate far earlier than previously known.

The group's members included senior scientists and engineers from nearly every major U.S. and multinational oil and gas company, including Exxon, Mobil, Amoco, Phillips, Texaco, Shell, Sunoco, Sohio as well as Standard Oil of California and Gulf Oil, the predecessors to Chevron, according to internal documents obtained by InsideClimate News and interviews with the task force's former director.

An InsideClimate News investigative series has shown that Exxon launched its own cutting-edge CO_2 sampling program in 1978 in order to understand a phenomenon it suspected could harm its business. About a decade later, Exxon spearheaded campaigns to cast doubt on climate science and stall regulation of greenhouse gases. The previously unpublished papers about the climate task force indicate that API, the industry's most powerful lobbying group, followed a similar arc to Exxon's

58

in confronting the threat of climate change.

Just as Exxon began tracking climate science in the late 1970s, when only small groups of scientists in academia and the government were engaged in the research, other oil companies did the same, the documents show. Like Exxon, the companies also expressed a willingness to understand the links between their product, greater CO_2 concentrations and the climate, the papers reveal. Some corporations ran their own research units as well, although they were smaller and less ambitious than Exxon's and focused on climate modeling, said James J. Nelson, the former director of the task force.

"It was a fact-finding task force," Nelson said in an interview. "We wanted to look at emerging science, the implications of it and where improvements could be made, if possible, to reduce emissions."

The group was initially called the CO_2 and Climate Task Force, but changed its name to the Climate and Energy Task Force in 1980, Nelson said.

A background paper on CO_2 informed API members in 1979 that carbon dioxide in the atmosphere was rising steadily, and it predicted when the first clear effects of climate change might be felt, according to a memo by an Exxon task force representative.

In addition, API task force members appeared open to the idea that the oil industry might have to shoulder some responsibility for reducing CO_2 emissions by changing refining processes and developing fuels that emitted less carbon dioxide.

Bruce S. Bailey of Texaco offered "for consideration" the idea that "an overall goal of the Task Force should be to help develop ground rules for energy release of fuels and the cleanup of fuels as they relate to CO_2 creation," according to the minutes of a meeting on Feb. 29, 1980.

The minutes also show that the task force discussed a "potential area" for research and development that called for it to "'Investigate the Market Penetration Requirements of Introducing a New Energy Source into World Wide Use.' This would include the technical implications of energy source changeover, research timing and requirements."

Yet by the 1990s, it was clear that API had opted for a markedly different approach to the threat of climate change. It joined Exxon, other fossil fuel companies and major manufacturers in the Global Climate Coalition (GCC), a lobbying group whose objective was to derail international efforts to curb heat-trapping emissions. In 1998, a year after the Kyoto Protocol was adopted by countries to cut fossil fuel emissions, API crafted a campaign to convince the American public and lawmakers that climate science was too tenuous for the United States to ratify the treaty.

"Unless 'climate change' becomes a non-issue, meaning that the Kyoto proposal is defeated and there are no further initiatives to thwart the threat of climate change, there may be no moment when we can declare victory for our efforts," according to the draft Global Climate Science Communications Action Plan circulated by API.

API and GCC were victorious when George W. Bush pulled the U.S. out of the Kyoto agreement. A June 2001 briefing memorandum records a top State Department official thanking the GCC because Bush "rejected the Kyoto Protocol in part, based on input from you."

API did not respond to several requests for comment on this story.

The Climate and Energy Task Force continued until at least 1983, when Nelson left API after a four-year stint. At the time, the Environmental Protection Agency's authority was growing, and oil companies believed the agency was silencing them, Nelson said. It became harder for corporations to get scientific papers published or to draw favorable media attention, the industry felt. In the end, company leaders feared this would lead to overregulation.

As a result, API decided that it wasn't enough to have scientists meeting in a task force about climate change or other pollution issues. It needed lobbyists to influence politicians on environmental issues, Nelson said.

"They took the environmental unit and put it into the political department, which was primarily lobbyists," Nelson said of API. "They weren't focused on doing research or on improving the oil industry's impact on pollution. They were less interested in pushing the envelope of science and more interested in how to make it more advantageous politically or economically for the oil industry. That's not meant as a criticism. It's just a fact of life."

Nelson said he departed API because he was not a lobbyist, but said he did not object to API's lobbying. Nelson does not accept that human activity is the main driver of climate change; he believes that natural cycles and phenomena such as volcanoes and deforestation have contributed significantly to a warming planet. The API was not about "trying to distort the truth but about getting the information out in a factual manner. It wasn't about propaganda," he said.

Nelson joined API in 1979 after a career as an Air Force pilot and then as the director of the first air quality monitoring system in Fairfax County, Va. At the time, API had an environment division that helped member companies organize and staff committees on potential pollution issues, including waste management and water quality. Nelson was hired to run the air quality committee, which focused largely on pollution such as sulfur dioxide, nitrogen oxides and other pollutants that had more immediate, local consequences.

CO_2 was not among the most pressing issues that API members faced, Nelson said. Still, by the time he arrived, companies were already putting together the task force to monitor the emerging science on higher atmospheric CO_2 concentrations and their possible impact on the climate. They had seen how pollution had hammered other industries, such as acid rain's effect on power generation or asbestos on construction, Nelson said. The oil industry did not want to be blindsided by the CO_2 problem, which the science of the late 1970s had already linked to fossil fuel combustion.

As the group came together, Raymond J. Campion, a scientist at Exxon Research and Engineering and a member of the task force, recommended in memos to colleagues that "CO_2 not receive a high priority" from API. One reason, Campion wrote, was because "the industry's credibility on such issues is not high at the present time, and should an API study indicate no serious CO_2 problems, the results would be greeted with skepticism."

Some of the recipients of those memos were top people on the lobbying and planning side of Exxon USA, the company's domestic affiliate. On July 9, 1979, Campion wrote a memo to W.W. Madden, the manager of strategic planning at Exxon USA. Campion noted "Bill Slick's need for information on atmospheric CO_2 buildup as a potential emerging issue for API to consider." Slick was an Exxon USA vice president and a well-known lobbyist in Washington.

Another reason to pursue a limited agenda, Campion wrote, was because the Energy Department and the American Association for the Advancement of Science (AAAS) were expected to issue a report "momentarily" based on an April 1979 climate symposium that "concluded no catastrophic hazards would be associated with the CO_2 buildup over the next 100 years and that society can cope readily with whatever problems ensue."

(Eventually published in October 1980, the AAAS report offered more sobering forecasts than Campion had expected, describing risks to nearly every facet of life on Earth and concluding catastrophes could be avoided only if timely steps were taken to address climate change.)

A memo from Campion to colleague J.T. Burgess dated Sept. 6, 1979 showed that the task force moved quickly to draft a background paper about CO_2. Campion wrote that he was asked to critique it for Slick to use in API discussions.

Campion suggested corrections to the background paper's quantification of the rate of CO_2 build-up, as well as an estimate in the paper that the "warming of the atmosphere…may be noticeable within the next twenty years."

He estimated that the effects would be felt after 2000, after a cyclical cooling period had passed. Because a cyclical warming trend was then expected post 2000, it would intensify climate change, "worsening the effect," he wrote. It is not known if the corrections were made to the paper.

Campion declined to be interviewed regarding his participation on the task force. Other Exxon representatives included Robert J. Fritz, who could not be located, and Henry Shaw, the company's lead climate researcher in the late 1970s, who is deceased. Exxon did not answer a request for comment.

The company representatives were scientists and engineers, and well-versed on air quality issues, Nelson recalled. Their views on carbon dioxide's possible impact on the climate varied, with many skeptical that man-made emissions could substantially affect the atmosphere. But they approached their participation on the task force dispassionately, he said.

"The individuals I had on the task force were very, very technically and ethically moral," Nelson said. "They felt that their job for their company was to look at an issue and if there was a problem, or if the petroleum industry was part of it or could contribute to fixing the problem, they wanted to do that."

Nelson organized the monthly meetings, took minutes and disseminated information companies wanted to share. Documents show representatives of about a half-dozen companies at various meetings. The meeting sites rotated among the members' cities, including oil hubs such as Houston and Tulsa; Washington, where API is located; and New York, where Exxon was headquartered at the time.

As Campion had recommended, API did not conduct its own research. But some of its members did, and they were generous about sharing their work and insights, Nelson said. "There were lots of discussions about climate models: whose were right and whose were wrong," he said.

Chevron acquired Texaco in 2000. Nelson said that Texaco's Bailey ran a small climate modeling team at the research facility in Beacon, N.Y. Bailey could not be located for comment. Chevron declined to comment on early CO_2 research activities.

At Shaw's urging, the task force invited Professor John A. Laurmann of Stanford University to brief members about climate science at the February 1980 meeting in New York. Shaw and Laurmann had participated in the same panel at the AAAS climate conference in April 1979.

Like many scientists at the time, Laurmann openly discussed the uncertainties in the evolving climate research, such as the limited long-term sampling data and the difficulty of determining regional effects of climate change, according to a copy of his presentation attached to the meeting minutes.

Still, Laurmann told his audience several times that the evidence showed that the increase in atmospheric CO_2 is likely "caused by anthropogenic release of CO_2, mainly from fossil fuel burning."

In his conclusions section, Laurmann estimated that the amount of CO_2 in the atmosphere would double in 2038, which he said would likely lead to a 2.5 degrees Celsius rise in global average temperatures with "major economic consequences." He then told the task force that models showed a 5 degrees Celsius rise by 2067, with "globally catastrophic effects."

The documents also show that the Energy Department contacted the task force in November 1979 to get its opinion on a study to be published in the journal Science about CO2 emissions from the development of oil shale. The government and oil industry had embarked on a mission to develop synthetic petroleum from sources such as oil shale and coal because of falling conventional oil production in the U.S. and political instability in the Middle East.

The Science study, by two geologists from the U.S. Geological Survey, estimated that synthetic crude from oil shale would generate three to five times more CO_2 than conventional oil, double previous estimates, the Energy Department said.

The task force spent several months analyzing and refining its statement on the USGS paper, documents show. "Our estimates are less than theirs," Nelson said, "and if their numbers become gospel and no one challenges them, it could cause concern."

Because it was heavily involved in synfuels, Exxon weighed in first in December 1979. Shaw said that the paper was well-written. But he agreed with the Energy Department that the CO_2 estimates were too high, and that "the paper may alarm the public unjustifiably," he wrote in a letter to API.

Shaw's own calculations about CO_2 from synfuels served as the basis of the eventual position paper the task force sent to the Energy Department in the spring of 1980 after multiple drafts. In one draft, the task force stated in March 1980 that the estimates in the Science article were accurate in light of the assumptions it used. "However, several of these assumptions stem from worst-case scenarios that are highly improbable and unrealistic," the task force concluded.

It is unclear what the Energy Department did with the task force's assessment of the paper. Roger C. Dahlman, the Energy Department staff member who sent the article to the task force, did not respond to multiple requests for comment.

After he left API in 1983, Nelson said he followed sporadically the organization's response to climate change. He said he felt the API's lobbying stemmed from a desire to have its concerns heard.

"That was the driving force, a worry about excessive regulation, my impression from having watched it along the way," he said.

Charles DiBona served as president of API from 1979 to 1997, when the organization shifted its approach on climate change from following the science to intense lobbying to discredit it. DiBona said in a phone interview that he did not remember the climate task force. Like Nelson, he does not accept the prevailing scientific consensus that climate change is being driven by fossil fuel combustion. "I think there is some question about the broader scientific community. There's not much evidence that there is real consensus," DiBona said.

In the 1990s, API argued that the science was too weak to warrant action, even as research grew more certain about the link between fossil fuel use, greater CO2 concentrations and rising global temperatures. Exxon chief executive Lee Raymond was API chairman from 1996 to 1997, when he focused on the uncertainty. The GCC emphasized the issue, too, in its public statements.

"Many people, politicians and the public alike, believe that global warming is a rock-solid certainty," Raymond said in a 1997 speech in Beijing. "But it's not."

API organized industry resistance to the possibility of the EPA's regulation of greenhouse gases in 1999. When the Bush administration took office, former API lobbyist Philip A. Cooney became chief of staff at the Council on Environmental Quality, the White House office that drove climate policy. Government scientists accused Cooney of rewriting federal research reports to sow doubt about man-made climate change. Cooney resigned in 2005 and went to work for ExxonMobil.

API's current position is that "fossil fuel development and environmental progress are not mutually exclusive," according to Jack Gerard, the group's president. But API still rejects any federal mandates to reduce greenhouse gas emissions. Gerard decried President Obama's Clean Power Plan to cut emissions from the country's power plants, the cornerstone of the administration's climate agenda, as destructive "government interference" in free markets.

APPENDIX I: LIST OF DOCUMENTS

Available for download at insideclimatenews.org

• **Government Meeting Memo (1977)**
Exxon scientist Henry Shaw summarizes a government meeting he attended, on the "global environmental effects of carbon dioxide."

• **James Black Talk (1977)**
Summary of a presentation on the CO_2 greenhouse effect that Black gave to top Exxon executives and other company scientists.

• **"Bad News" Letter (1978)**
Exxon scientist Henry Shaw tells his boss the company needs a "credible" team to research CO_2.

• **"Worldwide" R&D Memo (1978)**
Exxon's Harold Weinberg proposes some "grandiose thoughts" on how Exxon might research the "CO_2 problem."

• **CO_2 and Fuel Use Projections (1979)**
Exxon intern Steve Knisely's report on how global warming might affect future fuel use.

• **Comments on API CO_2 Research (July 1979)**
Exxon's Raymond Campion's memo about the American Petroleum Institute's CO_2 research strategy, July 1979.

• Comments on API CO2 Paper (Sept. 1979)
Exxon's Raymond Campion comments on the American Petroleum Institute's background paper on CO2 effects.

• Presentation to NOAA (1979)
Exxon and Columbia University scientists present their CO2 research plan to NOAA scientist Lester Machta.

• Probable Legislation Memo (1979)
Exxon scientist Henry Shaw tells his boss there is "a good probability" that CO2 legislation will eventually be passed.

• AQ-9 Task Force Meeting (1980)
The American Petroleum Institute's "CO2 and Climate Task Force" (AQ-9) meeting minutes from March 18, 1980.

• CO2 Forecast (1980)
Overview of the current scientific understanding of the CO2 greenhouse effect and ongoing federal research programs into the issue.

• Exxon's Policy Input to Congressional Commission (1980)
An Exxon researcher played a role as a Congressionally mandated commission examined policy options.

• Letters to Senior VPs (1980)
Exxon scientists update Senior Vice Presidents M.E.J. O'Loughlin and George T. Piercy on the status of their CO2 research.

• PR Plan for Exxon's CO2 Research (1980)
Exxon officials proposed a publicity campaign to burnish the company's image as a climate science leader.

• Weinberg CO2 Memo (1980)
Exxon's Harold Weinberg questions the concentration of CO2 in the ocean versus the atmosphere in a letter to his colleagues.

• "Catastrophic" Effects Letter (1981)
Exxon's Roger Cohen says the impacts of rising CO2 will likely be catastrophic.

• Exxon Position on CO2 (1981)
A brief summary of Exxon's position on the global warming in 1981.

• Exxon Review of Climate Research Program (1981)
In this scoping study, an Exxon manager recommends curtailing the company's ambitious climate research agenda.

• Gilbert Gervasi's Natuna CO2 Calculations (1981)
After examining a colleague's estimates of the CO2 that might be released from the Natuna gas field, Gervasi, the Natuna project manager, produced "more rigorous" calculations of the project's CO2 footprint.

• Budget Cutting Memo (1982)
A memo announcing Exxon's decision to slash its CO2 budget.

• "Consensus" on CO2 Impacts (1982)
Exxon's Roger Cohen says there's a "consensus" that a doubling of atmospheric CO2 concentrations will result in an average global temperature increase of roughly 3C.

• Esso Project Terminated (1982)
A letter announcing the termination of Exxon's CO2 project aboard the Esso Atlantic tanker.

• Exxon CO2 Primer (1982)
This document describes the state of the science on the greenhouse effect was widely circulated among Exxon management.

• Exxon Modeling (1982)
Presentation by Andrew Callegari on Exxon modeling results that reject Reginald Newell's conclusions.

• Natuna Background Paper (1983)
A background paper on the Natuna gas field's environmental issues.

• Natuna Environmental Concerns Letter (1983)
Alvin M. Natkin, Exxon's manager of environmental affairs, says the CO2 must be disposed of in a way that wins the approval of environmental groups.

• CO2 Sparging Report (1984)
Exxon Corporate Research investigates bubbling CO2 from the Natuna gas field into the ocean to prevent its release into the atmosphere.

• Exxon Climate Modeling (1984)
Presentation by Exxon scientist Andrew Callegari on Exxon's climate

modeling research.

• Shaw Climate Presentation (1984)
A 1984 conference presentation called "CO2 Greenhouse and Climate Issues" by Exxon scientist Henry Shaw.

• CO2 Research Update (1985)
Exxon scientist Brian Flannery reviews the company's climate change research efforts in a presentation.

• Handout For Meeting With Lee Raymond (1985)
Excerpts from a document that includes information on how Corporate Research interacts with the rest of Exxon. Includes data on CO2 and Natuna.

• Global Climate Science Communications Plan (1998)
The American Petroleum Institute's draft Global Climate Science Communications Plan from 1998.

• Exxon Lobbyist's Memo to the White House (2001)
Exxon's top lobbyist urged the White House to replace holdovers from the Clinton-Gore administration, accusing them of political bias.

• Global Climate Coalition Meeting (2001)
A 2001 State Department briefing memo about a meeting with representatives of the Global Climate Coalition.

• Exxon Scientist Lobbies the White House (2002)
Exxon's leading climate scientist worked to overhaul the Bush-Cheney administration's climate research strategy, focusing on uncertainty.

• MacCracken Letter to Exxon (2002)
In 2002, Michael MacCracken, the government's top climate scientist, wrote ExxonMobil's board chairman a scathing letter about the company's stance on climate science.

• Exxon Reply to the Royal Society (2006)
Ken Cohen, head of public and government affairs at Exxon, defended the company's record on climate change.

• Royal Society Letter to Exxon (2006)
Bob Ward, the Royal Society's communications director, complained that Exxon was distorting the science of climate change.

• McCarthy Exxon Statement (2007)

James McCarthy, a Harvard scientist, board member of the Union of Concerned Scientists and president-elect of the American Association for the Advancement of Science, testified in 2007 about Exxon's campaign of uncertainty at a congressional hearing.

APPENDIX II: CHARACTERS

• **James F. Black:** Black (1919-1988) was the Scientific Advisor in the Products Research Division of Exxon Research & Engineering, and one of the top technical people at Exxon Research & Engineering until his retirement in 1983. In 1977, Black told Exxon's management committee of top executives that emerging science showed that carbon dioxide levels were rising, likely driven by fossil fuel use, and such increases would boost global temperatures, leading to widespread damage.

• **Wallace Broecker:** As a Columbia University scientist, Broecker collaborated with Exxon on its climate research starting in the late 1970s through the mid-1980s. Working with Exxon's Henry Shaw, Broecker and his colleague Taro Takahashi helped analyze the carbon dioxide data collected from the company's tanker project. Nicknamed the "Grandfather of Climate Science," Broecker has received numerous awards for his research focused on the ocean's role in climate change, including the National Medal of Science in 1996. Broecker is a scientist with Columbia's Lamont-Doherty Earth Observatory, where he's been since 1959. He is also the Newberry Professor of Geology at Columbia.

• **Andrew Callegari**: After joining Exxon in 1980, Callegari took over the company's CO2 research efforts in 1981 and oversaw its climate modeling program. He served as Brian Flannery's boss and recruited New York University's Martin Hoffert as a consultant to help with the company's climate research. Callegari spent more than two decades at the oil company, where he worked across divisions from Exxon Research and Engineering to Exxon Mobil Corporation. Since 2007, he has worked as an energy consultant. In an interview with InsideClimate News, Hoffert described Callegari and Flannery as "very legitimate research guys."

• **Roger Cohen:** As a scientist at Exxon, Cohen spent the 1980s contributing to the company's climate research. During that time, he once described the predicted future impacts of climate change as "catastrophic" for most people on Earth. Cohen worked at Exxon for approximately 25 years, retiring in 2003 as a manager of strategic planning. After leaving the company, he became an outspoken climate denier. He helped lead the push for the American Physical Society to weaken its stance on the issue. In an article published in 2008, Cohen wrote: "...at the time of my retirement I was well convinced, as were most technically trained people, that the Intergovernmental Panel on Climate Change's case for Anthropogenic Global Warming (AGW) is very tight. However, upon taking the time to get into the details of the science, I was appalled at how flimsy the case really is." Cohen currently serves on the board of directors for CO2 Coalition, a group established in 2015 to counter "the demonizing of CO2 and fossil fuels."

• **Edward E. David:** David served as president of Exxon Research and Engineering (ER&E) in Florham Park, NJ from 1977 to 1986, when Exxon launched its own research into carbon dioxide from fossil fuel combustion and its effects on the global climate. From 1950 to 1970, he worked at Bell Laboratories, eventually becoming executive director of research. He served as the White House science advisor to President Richard M. Nixon from 1970 to 1973. David signed off on a groundbreaking Exxon project that used one of its oil tankers to gather atmospheric and oceanic carbon dioxide samples, beginning in 1979. He also oversaw the transition Exxon made to greater climate modeling. David kept Exxon upper management apprised of ER&E's carbon dioxide research. After retiring, David became a climate change denier. David was one of the 16 co-authors of an opinion piece deriding global warming that ran in the Wall Street Journal in 2012.

• **Brian Flannery:** Flannery was one of Exxon's top climate modelers after he joined the company in 1980. His research initially confirmed the findings of independent scientists, who said a doubling of CO2 in the atmosphere would raise average global temperatures by roughly 3 degrees Celsius. By 1990, however, Flannery served as Exxon's top scientific spokesman as it worked to derail international efforts to cut greenhouse gases from fossil fuel use. In 1998, he transitioned into a managerial role at ExxonMobil Corporation. Flannery spent three decades at the company; during that time, he served as a lead author of the Intergovernmental Panel on Climate Change's Working Group 3 (from 1998-2004) and was a member of multiple climate-related business committees. He continues to participate in the climate discussion as a fellow at Resources for the Future, an economic research and analysis nonprofit in Washington, D.C.

• **Clifton Garvin:** Garvin was Exxon's chairman and chief executive in the late 1970s and early 1980s, when the company was launching its ambitious climate-related tanker and modeling efforts. In a 1984 speech he made at Vanderbilt University, Garvin said the then-called "greenhouse effect" would "presumably lead to an increase in global temperatures with attendent consequences." Garvin worked at the oil company for nearly four decades. After retiring in 1986, he has held many roles from serving on the board of several major companies to participating on President Ronald Reagan's National Productivity Advisory Committee.

• **Edward Garvey:** Garvey worked at Exxon Research & Engineering from 1978 to 1983 and was Henry Shaw's top researcher on the tanker initiative. Exxon paid in part for his graduate studies at Columbia University; during that time, Garvey worked with Columbia University's climate researchers Wallace Broecker and Taro Takahashi. After leaving Exxon, Garvey has worked for various consulting firms and his main client has been the U.S. Environmental Protection Agency.

• **Martin Hoffert:** Martin Hoffert worked as a physics professor at New York University from 1975 to 2007. In that role, he teamed up with Exxon scientists Brian Flannery, Andrew Callegari and Haroon Kheshgi in the 1980s to review and create climate models. Hoffert said the collaboration during the 1980s was a good one. "We talked about the politics of this stuff a lot, but we always separated the politics from the science," Hoffert told InsideClimate News.

• **Mike MacCracken:** MacCracken was the scientific director for the climate unit of the U. S. Department of Energy's Carbon Dioxide Research and Assessment Program from 1979 to 1990. In that capacity, MacCracken helped coordinate various studies in the early 1980s by scientists from academia, government and the industry, primarily Exxon, into the potential climatic effects of increasing carbon dioxide. He is now Chief Scientist for Climate Change Programs with the Climate Institute, a non-governmental organization based in Washington D.C. that promotes national and international efforts to understand, adapt to and mitigate climatic change.

• **Maurice Edwin James "Morey" O'Loughlin:** O'Loughlin (1922-2009) served as a senior vice president and director of Exxon Corporation in the 1980s until his retirement in 1987. He took an interest in research by Exxon and outside scientists into the "greenhouse effect," as climate change was then known.

• **George T. Piercy:** Piercy (1915-2000) was an Exxon senior vice president in the late 1970s until his retirement in 1981. He was among the top executives regularly updated about the company's climate-related research. In the early 1970s, he served as the company's chief representative in negotiations with Middle Eastern countries during the Arab oil embargo and he oversaw the diversification of Exxon Enterprises. After Exxon, he worked as the chairman of the Education Broadcasting Corporation in New York and served on the boards of several nonprofit organizations.

• **Lee Raymond:** Raymond became the company's chief executive in 1993 and then added the position of chairman in 1999. He joined Exxon in 1963. Raymond was an outspoken skeptic of mainstream climate science. Under Raymond, Exxon led a coalition of fossil fuel companies called the Global Climate Coalition, which sought to delay action on climate change and cloud public understanding of the issue. Raymond retired in 2005 and was succeeded by Rex Tillerson.

• **Henry Shaw:** As manager of the Environmental Area in Exxon Research & Engineering's Technology Feasibility Center, Shaw (1934-2003) was one of the earliest employees to advocate for company research into atmospheric carbon dioxide levels. Shaw's family fled France in 1940 when the Nazis invaded. They eventually arrived in Brooklyn when Shaw was an adolescent. He joined Exxon in 1967. Shaw established a collaboration with Columbia University's Lamont-Doherty Geological Observatory, with which he developed the idea of outfitting a company oil tanker with special equipment to sample carbon dioxide concentrations in the air and water. Shaw left Exxon in 1986, to become a professor of chemical engineering at New Jersey Institute of Technology.

• **Taro Takahashi:** Takahashi, a climate scientist at Columbia University's Lamont-Doherty Earth Geological Observatory since 1957, collaborated with Exxon researchers on the company's ocean-related climate research in the late 1970s and early 1980s. Specifically, Takahashi and his colleague Wallace Broecker helped analyze the carbon dioxide data from air and ocean samples collected as part of the company's tanker project. Takahashi used the Exxon tanker data—along with dozens of datasets from universities and other research institutions—in two studies published in 1990 and 2009. He won the U.N. Environmental Programme's 2010 "Champion of the Earth" award for his climate-ocean studies. Takashi currently serves as Columbia's Ewing Lamont Research Professor.

• **Harold N. Weinberg:** Weinberg (1929-2008) ran Exxon Research & Engineering's Technology Feasibility Center in the early 1980s, the unit responsible for finding commercial applications for the studies scientists performed. In 1978, he proposed that Exxon launch a worldwide 'CO2 in the Atmosphere' research program. That did not materialize, but he remained active in the company's global warming studies. After retiring from Exxon in 1987, he became Vice President of Engelhard Corporation and later the Chairman of New Jersey's Institute for Energy Research, among other positions.

• **N. Richard Werthamer:** Werthamer worked at Exxon from 1978 to 1983, where he helped oversee the tanker research program. From 1980 to 1981, he was a manager at Exxon Research & Engineering and the boss of scientist Henry Shaw. Werthamer told InsideClimate News, "The whole idea was to do a really clean, really defensible research project, and that would be the key to open the door to whole [climate change] debate. It was for the company not to be the bad guy. Obviously later, the Exxon chairman and senior executives were climate deniers. That was not the case then." After leaving the company in 1983, he wrote a book on blackjack and served as executive director of the Becton, Dickinson and Company.

APPENDIX III: RELATED STORIES

(EDITOR'S NOTE: These stories can be found at insideclimatenews.org)

Exxon, Chevron Reject Shareholder Measures on Climate Change Again, by Elizabeth Douglass, May 28, 2015

Exxon's Gamble: 25 Years of Rejecting Shareholder Concerns on Climate Change, by Elizabeth Douglass, June 8, 2015

Exxon's 25 Years of 'No': A Timeline of Resolutions on Climate Change, by Elizabeth Douglass, June 8, 2015

Email Shows Exxon Was Studying Its Climate Impact in the '80s, by Neela Banerjee, July 8, 2015

Video: Exxon Researched Climate Change in 1977, in collaboration with FRONTLINE, Sept. 16, 2015

ExxonMobil Faces Heightened Risk of Climate Litigation, Its Critics Say, by Bob Simison, Sept. 30, 2015

Two U.S. Representatives Seek Justice Department Inquiry into Exxon, by David Hasemyer, Oct. 16, 2015

Bill McKibben Wants Everyone to Know Why He's So Mad at Exxon, by Katherine Bagley, Oct. 19, 2015

Sanders Calls for Investigation of 'Potential Corporate Fraud' by Exxon, by Lisa Song, Oct. 20, 2015

U.S. Senators Press Exxon for Answers on Climate Denial Funding, by John H. Cushman Jr., Oct. 29, 2015

How Exxon Overstates the Uncertainty in Climate Science, by John H. Cushman Jr., Oct. 29, 2015

Hillary Clinton Joins Call for Justice Dept. to Investigate Exxon, by Katherine Bagley, Oct. 29, 2015

Partnership with Exxon Puts MIT's Climate Action Vow to the Test , by Zahra Hirji, Oct. 29, 2015

Environmental and Civil Rights Groups Urge Federal Probe of Exxon, by Katherine Bagley, Oct. 30, 2015

Congressmen Call on SEC to Investigate Exxon's Climate Disclosures, by Neela Banerjee, Nov. 2, 2015

Congressmen Call on SEC to Investigate Exxon's Climate Disclosures, by Neela Banerjee, Nov. 2, 2015

Exxon CEO Denies Misleading Public About Climate Change, by John H. Cushman Jr., Nov. 5, 2015

New York Attorney General Subpoenas Exxon on Climate Research, by Bob Simison, Nov. 5, 2015

Subpoena Power: Exxon's Climate Scandal Now Under a Spotlight, by Zahra Hirji, Nov. 6, 2015

Peabody Settlement Shows Muscle of Law Now Aimed at Exxon, by David Hasemyer, Nov. 10, 2015

How We Got the Exxon Story, by Neela Banerjee, Nov. 10, 2015

Investors Urge Exxon to Take Moral Responsibility for Global Warming, by David Hasemyer, Nov. 11, 2015

Daniel Ellsberg: #ExxonKnew Is the Best 'Thank You' Since the Pentagon Papers, by David Sassoon, Nov. 15, 2015

350,000 Sign Petition Asking for Federal Probe of Exxon , by Katherine Bagley, Nov. 19, 2015

California Attorney General Urged to Investigate Exxon Over Climate, by David Hasemyer, Nov. 20, 2015

Exxon's Support of a Tax on Carbon: Rhetoric or Reality?, by David Hasemyer and Bob Simison, Dec. 21, 2015

APPENDIX IV: FRONTLINE VIDEOS

The PBS show "Frontline" produced a short film in collaboration with InsideClimate News about Exxon's early research into climate change to accompany our investigative series.

The film, as well as longer clips from interviews with Exxon researchers and InsideClimate News reporter Neela Banerjee, can be viewed at http://insideclimatenews.org/news/15092015/frontline-video

ABOUT THE AUTHORS

NEELA BANERJEE: Neela Banerjee is a Washington-based reporter for Inside Climate News. Before joining ICN, she spent four years as the energy and environmental reporter for the Los Angeles Times' Washington bureau. Banerjee covered global energy, the Iraq War and other issues with The New York Times. She also served as a Moscow correspondent with The Wall Street Journal. Ms. Banerjee graduated from Yale and grew up mostly in south Louisiana.

JOHN H. CUSHMAN JR.: Jack Cushman is the author of _Keystone and Beyond: Tar Sands and the National Interest in the Era of Climate Change_, which tells the definitive account of the Keystone XL pipeline saga. Before joining the InsideClimate News staff, he was a writer and editor in Washington, D.C. since 1978, principally with the Washington bureau of The New York Times. Cushman has written extensively about energy, the environment, industry and military affairs, also covering financial and transportation beats, and editing articles across the full spectrum of national and international policy.

Among his beat assignments at The Times, he covered climate and the environment during the Clinton administration. He served on the board of governors of the National Press Club and was its president in the year 2000. He has taught brief courses in media and environmental law at the Vermont Law School.

DAVID HASEMYER: InsideClimate News reporter David Hasemyer is co-author of the _Dilbit Disaster: Inside the Biggest Oil Spill You've Never Heard Of_, which won the 2013 Pulitzer Prize for National Reporting, was a finalist in the _2012 Scripps Howard Awards_ for Environmental Reporting and won an honorable mention in the 2012 John B. Oakes Award for Distinguished Environmental Journalism. Prior to joining InsideClimate News, he was a freelance journalist whose career included an award-winning tenure at the *San Diego Union-Tribune* as an investigative reporter. Hasemyer's work has been recognized by the Associated Press, the Society for Professional Journalists, the Society of American Business Editors and Writers and the California Newspaper Publishers Association. He has also been a finalist for the Gerald Loeb Award.

Among the articles Hasemyer researched and wrote for the *Union-Tribune* was a series about a 10-million ton pile of nuclear waste, a remnant of the uranium-mining boom in the 1950s and '60s that threatened the Colorado River. Those stories have been widely credited as critical to the U.S. Department of Energy's decision in 2000 to move the pile away from the river. Hasemyer graduated from San Diego State University with a Bachelor's degree in Journalism.

LISA SONG: Lisa Song joined InsideClimate News in January 2011, where she reports on oil sands, pipeline safety and natural gas drilling. She helped write "The Dilbit Disaster" series, which won the 2013 Pulitzer Prize for National Reporting, was a finalist in the 2012 Scripps Howard Awards for Environmental Reporting and won an honorable mention in the 2012 John B. Oakes Award for Distinguished Environmental Journalism. She previously worked as a freelancer, contributing to High Country News, Scientific American and New Scientist. Song has degrees in environmental science and science writing from the Massachusetts Institute of Technology.

INSIDECLIMATE NEWS

InsideClimate News is a Pulitzer prize-winning, non-profit, non-partisan news organization that covers clean energy, carbon energy, nuclear energy and environmental science—plus the territory in between where law, policy and public opinion are shaped. Our mission is to produce clear, objective stories that give the public and decision-makers the information they need to navigate the heat and emotion of climate and energy debates.

We have grown from a founding staff of two to a mature virtual newsroom of ten full time professional journalists and a growing network of contributors. We're aiming to double in size and come to full scale in the next two years.

Climate and energy are defining issues of our time, yet most media outlets are now hard-pressed to devote sufficient resources to environmental and investigative reporting. Our goal is to fill this growing national deficiency and contribute to the accurate public understanding so crucial to the proper functioning of democracy.

To help keep environmental journalism alive, donate to InsideClimate News by visiting:

https://donatenow.networkforgood.org/insideclimatenews

Manufactured by Amazon.ca
Bolton, ON

18999062R00050